CHAIRMAN CAZORT'S LITTLE RED BOOK OF WRITING

Also by Douglas Cazort:
Under the Grammar Hammer

CHAIRMAN CAZORT'S LITTLE RED BOOK OF WRITING

A Revolutionary Guide for Getting Better Grades

Douglas Cazort

Illustrations by Will Suckow

Lowell House
Los Angeles

Contemporary Books
Chicago

For Connie and Max Cazort
The Gang of Two

Library of Congress Cataloging-in-Publication Data
Cazort, Douglas.
    Chairman Cazort's little red book of writing : a revolutionary guide for getting better grades / Douglas Cazort.
        p. cm.
    ISBN 1-56565-074-3
    1. English language—Rhetoric.   2. Grading and marking (Students)   I. Title.
PE1408.C3928   1994
808'.042—dc20
                                                                                    93-21100
                                                                                         CIP

Requests for such permissions should be addressed to:
Lowell House
2029 Century Park East, Suite 3290
Los Angeles, CA 90067

Publisher: Jack Artenstein
Vice-President/Editor-in-Chief: Janice Gallagher
Director of Publishing Services: Mary D. Aarons
Text design: Hespenheide Design

Manufactured in the United States of America
10 9 8 7 6 5 4 3 2 1

STUDENTS IN ALL COURSES, UNITE!

CONTENTS

ACKNOWLEDGMENTS

I want to thank the many comrades who fought by my side during the writing and production of this book. For feedback and friendship, thanks to Cynthia Novak and Lee Ann Carroll of Pepperdine University, and Dick Finn of San Diego State University. Thanks also to the Seaver Dean's Office of Pepperdine for moral support of research and manuscript preparation. For creative and speedy work, a special thanks to the gung-ho comrades of the Pepperdine Word Processing Center, Jim Archibald, Darlene Kirtz, Jeneen Monteleone, Gem Rillwell, and Sue Bauer.

At Lowell House, credit goes to Comrade Bud Sperry, my editor, for his sense of humor and military timing (Hurry up and wait!), as well as partial credit for the title.

Finally, a large thank you to Peter Neumeyer of San Diego State University, whose seminar in the teaching of composition started me on my own Long March.

READ THIS FIRST!

If you picked up this book, there's a good chance you're worried about school writing. It may ease your worries to find out you're not alone. Research at UCLA by psychologist Morris Holland indicates that about 80 percent of all college students avoid courses, majors, and even careers that require writing, so you're in good company.

What's better, though, is the news that you can overcome your worries about the grade you'll make in any course that requires writing. The answer is in your hands, first in the lessons of this book, and then in the control you take over your grades (and future) through learning these lessons. Whether you're a freshman in high school or fresh into law school, whether you think you're a D writer or an uncertain A writer, you can expect to make better grades in any course requiring writing, and you can do it with less pain.

GETTING THE MOST FOR YOUR MONEY FROM THIS BOOK

First, read it through once, quickly. (It's a short book, hooray!) Even if you do nothing else, one reading will give you a full awareness of the special problems of school writing and how to overcome them. Then you'll know which parts of the book best suit your own needs, and you'll also know the direction to take to find the shortest road to an A on all your writing (and a higher GPA, the best colleges or grad schools, success, fame, fortune, happiness, etc.).

So, what are you waiting for?

Study Chairman Cazort's writings,
follow his teachings, and act
according to his instructions.

Lin Piao

CHAIRMAN CAZORT'S LITTLE RED BOOK OF WRITING

1

DID YOU SAY YOU WANT A REVOLUTION?

Well, maybe you didn't say it, but by reading this far, you have shown an interest in revolutionary methods that will improve your grades on writing. So let's get straight about what the revolution is against.

First, it is against a system of grading and red-marking, a system that oppresses your ability to write. As Professor Paul Diederich of the Educational Testing Service puts it, "The grade a paper gets depends on who grades it." And, according to Professor George Hillocks of the University of Chicago, when papers are marked for every error, the quality of student writing actually declines!

In addition to the system of grades and red marks, there's another revolution to be fought, and it's against inner enemies created by the outer system. Low grades, red marks, and harsh criticism of your papers have led many of you to fear the act of writing and to believe you can't write. If you're like the UCLA students who avoid writing, you'll have to root out these fears and beliefs before you'll even be willing to take courses that require writing. Then you'll be able to tackle the system that stands between you and better grades.

These are the outer and inner enemies in our revolutionary war. I'll describe them more fully as we go on, and I'll teach you the lessons of guerrilla writing you'll need to overthrow them. It will surprise you to find out how little you really need to know to win the wars of writing. What's important is what you do with what you learn.

CHAIRMAN MAO HAS GONE AWAY CHAIRMAN CAZORT IS HERE TO STAY

By now, this talk of revolution and guerrilla war may have made you nervous. Am I trying to turn you into an academic terrorist, waving the red banner and brandishing the hammer and sickle, or what? Am I saying that you will need to battle every teacher who grades every piece of your writing? No, comrades, not at all. In fact, I am a strong believer in the free enterprise system, apple pie, Mom, and the American Dream. Far from asking you to become a Red, I will show you how to defeat all things red: red pens, gory grammar hammers, and the bloody sickles of writing self-doubt.

Thus, the lessons of this book are designed to help you become a chairman or chairwoman of the board, not of the Communist Party. If you follow these lessons well, you'll learn how to fight the system I described above without fighting teachers who use it. Paradoxically, you'll actually become a student who will be welcome in any teacher's class.

For after all, as the great Chinese master Sun Tzu wrote two thousand years ago in *The Art of War:* ". . . the true object of war is peace." And peace, in your case, is the peace of mind that comes with knowing you can deal with a system that's stacked against you and yet still come out the victor.

So throw away your pictures of Chairman Mao, cut out the picture of Chairman Cazort and place it next to your heart, and march forward with confidence to win your own personal writing revolution.

Still with me? Have you bought the book? OK, from now on, you may call me Chairman Doug.

2

• •

THE MAKING OF A GUERRILLA WRITER

• •

Success in warfare is gained by carefully accommodating ourselves to the enemy's purpose.

Sun Tzu
The Art of War

L et me introduce you to a model for the role you need to play if you want to win your writing revolution. Karina is a recent graduate of Pepperdine University, and in the past few years, she has racked up quite an impressive record of writing. At Pepperdine, she wrote over forty major papers, and with the exception of the first two, the lowest grade she made on any of them was a B+.

During Karina's senior year in college, she worked fifteen hours a week for a Los Angeles law firm, researching legal cases and writing case summaries. This summer she will clerk for a district court judge, and once again, most of her time will be spent writing. Then in the fall, she will enter the law school of a prestigious West Coast university, where she was told that the strength of her writing was a deciding factor in her admission.

Yet Karina says that when she entered Pepperdine, she hated writing. Her first language was Spanish, and even though she went to school in the United States from the first grade onward, writing was never her strong point. Not only that, her initial writing experience at Pepperdine was a bad one. She

received a C– on the first two papers she turned in for a freshman seminar, even though she worked harder on them than she ever had for any paper she had written in high school. She had even received help with revision at the Pepperdine Writing Center before turning the papers in. Yet the teacher thought they were C– papers.

Then, between writing her second and third papers, Karina learned her first lesson in guerrilla writing and applied it. When she got the third paper back, it had received an A–. For the remainder of the course, Karina got an A– or an A on every paper, and she finished with a B+ in the course. What happened? Well, in all modesty, I have to tell you that Karina was also a student in my English composition class, and at the time her second paper got a C–, we were reading research on the subjective nature of essay grading, research that substantiates the claim that the grade a paper receives depends on who grades it.

Karina also learned what to do with this knowledge. She went directly to her teacher and asked him to read the rough draft of her third paper and tell her what she needed to do to revise it. He is a helpful teacher, so he did, and Karina followed his suggestions, rewrote the paper, and brought it back for additional advice. Then she typed up the final draft, took it to the Writing Center for a final check, and turned it in for an A–.

I want you to notice that Karina didn't argue about the grade, nor did she try to educate her teacher about the subjective nature of grading or try to get him to change his grading system. In fact, she didn't fight him in any way. Note also that the teacher was impressed with Karina's desire to write better, and he was glad to help her revise her paper.

Safe and simple, right? And the credit goes to Chairman Doug. Wrong. The credit goes to Karina for learning the lessons and acting on them. OK, if you insist, I'll take some of the credit. But over the years, I have provided hundreds of students with the information Karina had, yet too few of them have taken the trouble to put it into practice like Karina did in her college courses and in her legal writing.

So, is this all you need to learn to make better grades on your writing? Of course not. If it were, you wouldn't need to buy this book, and if you didn't, that would create serious consequences for my own quest for the American Dream (as well as your permission to call me Chairman Doug). But don't worry about that. As Karina did, you'll learn many lessons of guerrilla writing, and I hope that, like Karina, you will believe in their power and put them into practice. In the words of another chairman, Henry Ford, "Whether you believe you can or you can't, you're right."

So believe it, comrade grasshoppers, because you'll need both knowledge *and* belief when you do battle with the system that determines the grades on your writing, a system we will examine closely as soon as you turn the page.

3

●●●●●●●●●●●●●●●●●●●●●●●●●●●●●●●●●●●●●●

THE FIRST
LESSON OF WAR:
KNOW YOUR ENEMY

●●●●●●●●●●●●●●●●●●●●●●●●●●●●●●●●●●●●

**If you know the enemy and know yourself,
you need not fear the result of a hundred
battles.**

Sun Tzu
The Art of War

By this time in your life, you have taken many classes, and you know by now that teachers come in all shapes, sizes, and temperaments. It is good that you expect these differences, and even better if you learn to notice the individual quirks that have a bearing on your grade ("One mistake in a paper, and I give you a C. Two and I give an F!").

But with all these differences, all teachers share one characteristic in common: The grades they give to writing are influenced by their subjective bias. This is the first lesson you need to learn in order to make an A on all your writing. So, hang in there for the next few pages while I go into some detail about the surprising (and disturbing) ways teachers actually arrive at grades on writing. Then you'll be much better prepared for my advice about what to do when confronted with the teachers who will grade your writing.

FIRST, A SHORT TRUCE

By now you know that I will use the metaphor of war to describe your relationship with teachers who will grade your writing. And even though you may have already done battle with teachers over writing grades, this war metaphor might seem extreme and even scary as you face your next writing class. So I'm calling a short truce to reassure you.

Of course, teachers are not really your enemies, not even English teachers, who will grade the largest amount of your writing in high school and the first year of college. In fact, of all the types of teachers I have known, English teachers are probably the most conscientious as a group. They really care that their students learn to write better, and they spend many extra hours correcting papers to reach that goal. Unfortunately,

there are several reasons that their efforts backfire, creating the war footing that often exists between teacher and student.

First, many teachers do not read research on what works (or doesn't work) in the teaching of writing. Instead, they rely on untested practice handed down from the last generation of teachers. This leads to the major causes of war, the overcorrecting and too frequent grading of papers. As we have learned, some well-executed studies have found that correcting all errors in papers leads to a *decline* in the quality of student writing. In addition, research by Diederich and his associates found that grading every paper in a course is unnecessary and only contributes to conflict between teachers, students, and their parents.

If teachers spent less time grading and marking papers and more time conferencing with students, the war would wind down. However, this book isn't designed to change teachers or the system, but to provide you, the student, with methods for dealing with the system as it is, which in the area of grades is often a battle.

So as you read further, remember that the enemy I describe is only an enemy when it comes to grading your work, and then mainly because of misplaced zeal. Don't let that blind you to the ways in which your teachers have something unique and valuable to offer.

THE MINEFIELD OF WRITING GRADES

According to research done by the Educational Testing Service, when a group of English teachers grades a set of papers, on the average, 20 percent of the papers will receive every grade from A through F. And the disagreement increases to 30 percent if you include teachers in other disciplines among the graders. If this sounds like an item from Ripley's *Believe It or Not,* I'm not surprised. When I first read it, I didn't believe it, either. So I set up a small study in the English Department at San Diego State University to see if I could find results similar to Diederich's prediction.

I asked ten SDSU English teachers to participate in a workshop to grade eight papers written by my college English students. The papers were all written during the initial class period of the semester on the same topic, and I chose them at random from a set of about fifty. I asked the faculty members to read the papers and give them any letter grade from A through F, including plus and minus grades.

The paper that caused the greatest disagreement received grades from A through D, and another paper received grades from B+ through D–. That's two of the eight papers, so 25 percent received seven different grades with only ten graders grading. That was close enough to Diederich's findings to convince me (20 percent will receive every grade from A through F). The paper that caused the least disagreement among the graders received two A's, two B+'s, three B's and three B–'s. So the best grading is hardly what you'd call reliable.

Since I did that study, I have used the paper that received the grades from A through D in a bit of informal research. In various workshops on writing or grading, I have asked over 150 teachers of college English to grade it, as well as thirteen businesspeople and engineers at the General Atomic Company. The results are below, along with the original grades the paper received at SDSU:

		A	A–	B+	B	B–	C+	C	C–	D+	D	D–	F
10	SDSU Faculty	2	2	0	1	0	0	1	2	1	1	0	0
13	GA Employees	1	2	1	2	1	1	1	2	1	1	0	0
69	USC Instructors	4	6	15	11	11	4	7	7	0	2	1	1
81	USC Instructors (post rubric)	2	4	9	16	14	12	14	6	4	0	0	0

The last two sets of grades came from workshops for new instructors at the University of Southern California. I conducted the workshops over a period of four years, and one instructor in the second year's group protested that I should have first prepared the graders by giving them a set of guidelines for each grade, a "rubric," as it is called in this profession. So, for the next two years, I first supplied the instructors with the rubric used by their own department, one which they had already been trained to use in grading the waiver exam given at USC at the beginning of the semester (more about waiver exams in Appendix D).

As you will note, the rubric seems to have had some effect. Even though there are twelve more instructors in the post-rubric group, there are fewer grades at the extreme ends of the scale and more in the center, especially in the B to C range. However, even these instructors who had the benefit of prior rubric training gave the paper every grade from A through D+, so these results still don't represent the kind of system you could trust to determine your grade with an acceptable degree of objectivity or fairness. Unfortunately, that's the state of the art in the grading system today. Diederich's research was conducted before 1974, mine as recently as 1991, and I haven't read any research indicating that teachers have changed since then.

The problems with bias in grading don't stop here. Not only do teachers give the same paper different grades, they do so for reasons that defy explanation. Let me explain. When I asked instructors to grade the single paper, I also asked them to write down the two main reasons they chose the grade they did. For example, two simple statements like, "Good use of facts and nice introduction," or "Poor organization and awkward wording." I had thought that different graders would concentrate on different categories to give the paper different grades; in other words, one grader would focus on a weakness in the paper to give it a low grade, while another would notice a strength in the paper and give it a high grade.

But to my surprise, I found that many graders had utilized the very same categories to justify grading the paper at different ends of the scale. From the grades and responses of one group of graders, I isolated the following pairs of comments, each of which focuses on a similar category while drawing the opposite conclusion about the quality of its use. Remember, all the comments were made by people sitting in the same room, at the same time, reading the same paper.

HIGHER GRADERS	LOWER GRADERS
Excellent title	Poor title
Good opening—draws attention	Weak intro—misleading
He stuck with his opinion	Skipped around, left topic
Focus is consistent	Poor focus
Paragraphs run into each other well	Bad transitions between paragraphs
Very good sources; good examples and references	Unreliable sources, poor examples
Good development	Poor development
Good sentence structure	Bad sentence structure
Good word choice	Overly florid prose
Good vocabulary	Too large a vocabulary

In case you're curious about the kind of paper and assignment that would generate so much disagreement, I have included it in Appendix A. If you expect something bizarre, you'll probably be disappointed. The subject itself isn't really controversial, and the paper is just a paper—common college English variety. Yet in grading it, teachers, businesspeople, and engineers react in personal ways that are hard to explain, if not impossible.

However, I want to make it clear that I don't believe these reactions are the result of a conspiracy by evil teachers against innocent students. My own grading is no more objective than that of any other teacher, nor would yours be. It turns out that we react to school writing with as much variety as we do to novels, songs on the radio, or movies. Not everyone likes the same book, song, or movie equally, nor do we expect them to. The only problem is that most teachers don't realize that this same subjectivity applies to their response to your writing, and therefore they place too much weight on this all-too-human method of determining your grade.

Now, what does all this mean to you as you face the next teacher who will grade your writing? Do you have to just give up hope and take your punishment? No. Believe it or not, a teacher's natural bias can be influenced in your favor. To illustrate this possibility, here's one last word from research on grading.

EARNING HONORS IN THE WARS OF WRITING

In one of the studies conducted by the Educational Testing Service, separate groups of high school English teachers in two New York schools were given identical student papers to grade during the course of a school year—a new set of papers each month. The teachers didn't know who the students were or which schools they attended. However, they did know that some of the students were enrolled in honors writing sections, and they asked the researcher, Dr. Benjamin Rosner, to tell them which papers were written by honors students so they could grade them with tougher standards.

Dr. Rosner agreed to comply with the teachers' request, but what he did in reality was to choose writers at random and stamp their papers "honors." He continued this practice throughout the study, one month stamping a student's paper "honors," the next stamping it "regular." In this way, the graders saw the randomly chosen students' papers labeled "honors" half the time and "regular" the other half. Rosner found that these falsely identified "honors" papers received higher grades than the very same copies marked "regular" that were graded by the other group of teachers—on the average a full letter grade higher. This indicated that the teachers' perception of a paper as an honors paper influenced their grades in an upward direction, even though their stated intention was to grade it by tougher standards.

Diederich cites this as yet another example of teacher bias in grading, and what's important for you to note is his conclusion that once a teacher's perception of a student's writing is formed, it is difficult to change, especially when the perception is influenced by such additional factors as the personality and classroom performance of the student.

Diederich's research and observations are important because they contain the key to your making an A in writing courses, in spite of the biased nature of grades on writing. As you'll soon learn in following chapters, there are many methods for influencing a teacher's bias in your favor. In other words, you can perform the equivalent of stamping "honors" on your papers. At the same time, you will learn how to immunize yourself from negative effects caused by attacks on your writing. And finally, you will learn how to become a better and more comfortable writer, regardless of how your teacher reacts to your writing.

HOW THE OUTER ENEMY CREATES THE INNER ENEMY

And now, for something completely familiar, read this piece written by a freshman at Pepperdine University:

> English Composition—two words most of us had hoped we'd never run into again once we were handed that sacred high school diploma. I, for one, still have nightmares over some of the things I experienced back in Senior English Composition class. There's this one in particular where I'm receiving my essay back from my instructor. The instructor has two heads, six eyes and no ears. The paper is soaked in red ink and the only identifiable mark is this huge letter "F" across the top. I begin to whimper that I spent three weeks on this assignment, that I put my very heart and soul into the paper. The instructor, unable to hear my pleas, suddenly turns and is wielding this tremendous club with the word "grammar" boldly printed on the side. Within seconds, I find myself being hit repeatedly over the head with the club, and the beating continues for hours on end.
>
> I wake up in a pool of sweat, the memory of my real life teacher, Mrs. Carson, fresh in my mind. You can imagine, then, the anxiety I felt as I studied the list of required courses in my college handbook and found English Composition to be among them. It actually had me questioning whether a college education was really that important after all.

This does sound familiar, doesn't it? For most of you, it should. As I mentioned earlier, research at UCLA indicates that as many as 80 percent of college students have suffered enough bad experiences with writing that they avoid courses, majors, and even careers that require them to write. If you're a member of the 80 percent, it's no news to you that writing courses can be bad news. Unfortunately, the news gets worse.

THE AWFUL TRUTH ABOUT THE CAUSES OF WAR

An integral part of bad experiences with writing classes is the grade your writing receives, and the worst news of all is that, to a large degree, the grade a piece of writing gets depends upon who grades it. Now, wait. Did I say the worst news is that the grade your writing receives depends on who grades it? I guess I got ahead of myself. The absolute worst news is that every high school, college, and grad school in the United States requires you to take courses in which you have to write papers and essay exams that determine or influence your course grade.

At the heart of all these awful truths and bad news is the issue of control over your grades. In courses that require writing for a grade, you don't exert much control, at least not the kind of control you enjoy in courses where your grades are established by objective tests of your knowledge. Generally, in courses with objective exams, the harder you study, the higher the grade you can make on the tests. In other words, there's a fairly direct relationship between the amount of work you put into the course and the grade you receive.

In writing courses, however, the relationship between increased effort and a higher grade on your writing doesn't always exist. You can work hard all semester, yet end up with the grade you made on your very first paper. Or even if your grade improves over the semester, you can take a second semester of the same course with a different teacher and make a lower grade than you did the first semester. This can happen to you again and again throughout your high school and college career, until you become convinced you have little or no control over your writing grades.

This feeling of lack of control is crucial. Research with both animals and humans shows that the absence of control over desired outcomes can create a state of "learned helplessness" in which all our efforts to reach goals just disappear, and we become apathetic and depressed. The concept of learned helplessness was developed after years of research by Dr. Martin Seligman, a psychologist at the University of Pennsylvania. One of his experiments involved two groups of dogs. Each dog was put into a box with an electrified wire grid for a floor, but the dogs from one group were restrained in a harness that prevented their escaping from the box. Those from the other group were left free in the box, so that when they were shocked, they could escape. (See, those psychologists aren't all bad.)

When the restrained dogs learned that their actions didn't have any influence on any outcome, they would give up trying to escape and just lie down whimpering on the grid. Then, when put into the box without the harness and shocked, they would again lie down on the electrified grid, as if they were still restrained by the harness! They had learned helplessness with regard to escaping the electric shock.

Another experiment reported by Seligman involved creating helplessness in college students. The experimenters gave one group of students a problem to solve, but unknown to them, the problem had no solution. Another group of students was given a problem that could be solved. When both groups were given identical problems to solve, the members of the first group could not solve them. Those from the second group could.

If you'll think about the traditional writing course, you can see a similar situation to the ones that produced learned helplessness in the dogs and the students. Students write, turn in their writing, and get back the bad news. To see how the news affects them, let's look at an early study on the effects of negative comments and corrections that was performed on two groups of fourth graders matched for sex, IQ, and income level of their parents (see Taylor and Hoedt in the Bibliography).

Students in both groups were asked to write a theme every week for ten weeks in their science classes. One group's papers received written praise without any corrections. The other

group's papers were given critical written comments, and all errors were circled in red. At the end of the study, neither group differed in the rated quality of its work; however, the group that received criticism and corrections had written significantly less than the group receiving praise. Also, members of the criticized group were less willing to write again than those of the praised group. And, in answering a questionnaire about the experience, twenty-two of the fifty-two students in the criticized group answered that the critical written comments on their papers made them feel like giving up.

More recent research backs up these findings. Dr. George Hillocks at the University of Chicago found that when student papers are marked to correct every error, the quality of the students' writing declines. These results could mean that the students have given up hope that they will ever be able to improve their writing. This interpretation could easily follow from what we've seen about the effects of frustration on performance and the effects of absence of control over a desired outcome.

In other words, many of us have learned helplessness in the face of uncontrollable writing grades and red marks, so we avoid courses and majors that require writing, and thereby narrow our range of career choices.

Unfortunately, learning that we can't write doesn't stop in school. The strong negative responses to writing keep on coming in business, the military, and private life, especially in response to surface errors. In an Air Force manual on writing, there's a story about a colonel who ordered his clerks not to use white-out on typed communications, and he even had a special light box made so he could detect the more subtle white-overs done by self-correcting typewriters.

But with all the bad news, there is some good. Seligman did cure his helpless dogs. He dragged them over the electric grid to an opening in the box until they learned to get out on their own, even when they were put into different boxes. Seligman also managed to cure his students by revealing that he had given them unsolvable problems and then allowing them to practice with solvable problems. The same good news applied to the fourth graders. When the members of the criticized group were given the choice of writing again, but this time without negative comments or corrections from the teacher, they reversed their earlier decision not to write.

The best news of all is that the good news applies to your writing. That's right, friends and fledgling warriors, help is on the way. At this very moment, Chairman Doug is coming to the rescue at the speed of light, or at any rate, the speed it takes to read this book. Yes, you can learn to gain control over your grades in courses that require writing, and that's what this book is all about.

In the lessons ahead, you'll learn how to overcome teacher bias in grading, and you'll do it without wasting any time or energy trying to change the system of grading. You will also learn to overcome your own negative attitudes toward writing. Better still, you'll rarely be required to work harder, just smarter. Best of all, you'll learn the most important lessons quickly—this is, after all, a short book. I'll tell you all you need to know to make an A on all your writing, and nothing you don't need to know. Then it will be up to you to follow in the footsteps of Karina, the guerilla writer, and put your new knowledge into practice.

4

• •

A RUMOR OF WAR: WHAT TO DO BEFORE YOU HAND IN YOUR FIRST PAPER

• •

In times of peace, prepare for war.
Sun Tzu
The Art of War

All right, let's imagine the worst has happened. You have to take a course in which the teacher will grade your writing. The first day of class draws near, and you know you're stuck with this class for the duration. What can you do to defend your GPA from attack? As we learned in the last chapter, the first lesson is to know your enemy! You know about the system of grades and red marks; now get to know your teachers. Pay attention to their individual quirks and requirements. Treat them with the fear, respect, and watchfulness you would show to soldiers of a hostile army in unscouted terrain. Learn the danger signals, the warning signs, the odd habits, and the secret weapons that vary from teacher to teacher.

It's a sad fact that some teachers set up their classes so that minor requirements can exert an influence on your grade that is far out of proportion to their importance in teaching you to write. Some of these requirements will catch your attention right away ("Late papers get an F!"). Others, however, are more subtle and may even go unstated. In this chapter, I'll train you to recognize where most dangers lie and teach you how to avoid them. Even before you turn in your first paper, there are actions you can take to dance nimbly out of range before your enemy opens fire.

So, be warned. As you read the following pages, think about this first lesson, and always step with stealth and caution when you encounter members of the species who intend to grade your writing. Know that they are unpredictable. Learn to expect the unexpected. Then when it comes, you'll be able to meet it with grace under pressure, forewarned by your older comrade in arms (Chairman Doug) and your own rigorous habits of watchful attention.

In this chapter, you'll learn methods for raising your grade even before you hand in your first written assignment. Many of these may seem obvious, yet I see students who ignore them, thereby lowering their chances for a high grade even before they set foot in class. How could that be possible? I'll explain in detail in the following section, but for now, here's a sneak preview.

Almost every semester, I get at least one student in each class who doesn't show up for the first couple of classes and doesn't even bother to tell me why. What do you think this tells me about the student's attitude toward my class? And how do you think this affects my attitude toward the student? OK. So what's the lesson you learn from this short preview? Right! Be there or be square!

DON'T START THE WAR WITHOUT ME

I think it was Woody Allen who wrote that 90 percent of success is showing up for work. Attendance in class may not exert that strong of an effect on success, but the lack of it can provide a strong cause for failure. By the end of the first class session (and I'm assuming you'll be there), make sure you know your instructor's attendance requirements. Don't just assume

your instructor follows the school's policy. His or hers may be even more strict! And even if your college instructor claims not to care that much, if you show by your absence that you don't value what your instructor has to offer, you could very well hurt your grade.

It may be that you *don't* value your instructor or the course, but this way of showing it can bias your instructor against you, and we know by now what effect that can have on the way your instructor evaluates your writing. A far better way to show your dislike of a course is to take the waiver option described in Appendix D. However, if you tried that and it didn't work, then make the best of a bad situation and show up for every class. Whether or not you find anything of value there, at least you won't jeopardize your grade.

ON BEING FASHIONABLY LATE TO BATTLE

The next thing to find out about your instructor is his or her policy regarding lateness, both in regard to coming to class and turning in papers. Many instructors will make their attitude toward lateness clear. I know of one instructor in the cinema department at USC who locks his door and doesn't let latecomers in. Others may not mention lateness, but this doesn't mean it doesn't bother them. Being late to class can be especially annoying to an instructor who always discusses the assignment during the first few minutes of class. I'm one of those instructors, and when students miss my instructions, I always get the nagging feeling that I need to repeat the instructions for them so they'll get the assignment right. That's not a good feeling to inspire in your instructor, especially if you compound the lateness by doing the assignment incorrectly.

The same advice goes for turning in your papers on time. Some instructors I know won't accept a late paper for credit, counting it as zero when computing a student's average. Again, some teachers may have a lenient attitude toward late attendance or papers, but even "easy" teachers tend to feel taken advantage of by someone who consistently abuses their generosity. Don't be that someone! As always, the final word is, know your teacher's policy and follow it.

KNOW WHERE YOU ARE—KNOW WHERE YOU'RE GOING: FOLLOW DIRECTIONS

Imagine you are now sitting in class the first day. You came to class on time with pen and paper, prepared to write an in-class essay or just to take notes. Now, from the very first moment of class, learn to pay attention to your instructor. Listen to his or her instructions and follow them. If he or she hands out a syllabus or course description, read it immediately and make sure you understand everything in it. If your teacher discusses it in class, listen! Take notes. Ask questions to clear up anything you don't understand. The same goes for assignments. Read them more than once. If assignments are given orally or written on the board, take notes.

Make sure you always know exactly what your teachers want and give it to them. Otherwise, you run the risks of frustrating them in the minor ways that can lead to major bias against you and your writing. Let me give you some examples. Sometimes students turn in the wrong assignment, or they get the assignment right, but turn it in on the wrong day, even though they received the correct information in writing. Other times they interpret the assignment in such a way that it doesn't fulfill the requirements. When asked to reread the assignment sheet, they respond with statements that can drive an instructor (me) up the wall: "Oh, I should have read the instructions before I started to write." Or "I lost my copy but John said to write it this way." Or "I know you wanted it the other way, but I decided to be more creative."

Everyone makes mistakes, and it's no crime to lose an assignment sheet. But make sure you have made an honest effort to follow directions. Then the occasional slipup won't count as heavily as consistent mistakes made due to indifference. Look at it this way. All these messages from the instructor are your maps through unknown territory or enemy terrain. Ignoring them is tantamount to wandering through a minefield wearing a blindfold. However, knowing them with certainty and following them will help you negotiate the major obstacles to your goal at the far side of the course—an A on all your writing and an A in the course.

THE MAGICAL, TWO-WAY INTERROGATION MIRROR

When it comes to classroom behavior, most of the advice I could give would seem too obvious to mention. For example, everyone knows not to carry on a conversation with a fellow student while the instructor is talking, right? Right. Yet over the years, first as a student and then as an instructor, I have noticed a strange phenomenon in the classroom. Whenever a teacher begins to talk, it seems that a magical, two-way mirror descends between the teacher and the class, allowing students to see and hear the teacher, but not the reverse. Therefore, these students feel free to talk to their neighbors because the teacher can't see through the mirror.

As a student, I knew this feeling well, but to my surprise, when I began working on the other side of the mirror, its magic ceased to work! I could see my students when they talked, and I found it very distracting. So think of this: If I can see my students, then your teachers can see you, and if they are distracted by your talking, it could affect your grade.

Let me give you a specific example. I remember one student in the first class I ever taught who would read the newspaper during class or talk to the girl who always sat beside her. After I realized she wasn't going to stop on her own accord, I talked to her after class and told her what a distraction her behavior was. Surprisingly enough, she was quick to apologize and explain her actions. She said that the girl beside her was her best friend from high school, and because of jobs and different class schedules, this was the only time they got to talk together. Still, she said she realized that this wasn't the best time to catch up on her social life, and from now on, she'd find some out-of-class time for her conversations. Which she did, and which I appreciated.

Things don't always work out so well. Several years after that first class, I ran into a similar situation with another student. This time, when I discussed the problem with the student in conference, she said she would stop talking to her friend, but during the next class period, she kept up an on-again, off-again whispering. When I talked to her again, she said she forgot, and that really it was my fault for not reminding her during class. This isn't the kind of reaction I'd recommend to you if you're working to impress upon your teacher that you're A material.

Now, in both students' favor, I realize that they probably wouldn't have taken freshman English if they hadn't been forced to. Who would? Yet it just doesn't pay to show your anger or boredom by talking, reading newspapers, or otherwise distracting the teacher. Instead, try to find a method which helps you endure the class with some grace. Probably the most helpful action you could take for a better grade would be to develop an interest in the class. Take notes, even join in class discussions.

However, if that doesn't work, learn some form of meditation that allows you to keep your eyes open and glued to the teacher, while your brain travels in space and time. Practice memorizing math or chemistry formulas for exams. See how many important facts you can remember from your history readings. But save your newspapers and conversations for after class, and save yourself and your grade the possible grief.

SPIT AND POLISH—KNOW THE DRESS CODE

Even in modern armies, soldiers are required to spend a certain amount of time shining boots and polishing belt buckles. Learning these skills won't make them better fighters, but the regulations require it anyway. In school, there are parallel lessons that you have to learn, not about your personal appearance but the appearance of your writing. For example, some teachers may want to see your rough draft first, while others expect typed, flawless papers the first time around.

You need to find out your teacher's preference for the physical format and appearance of your papers and make sure you follow it. If all your papers have to be typed and corrected before submission, then type them and hand them in as mistake-free as possible. If you can't type or hate to, then spend the few dollars it costs to hire a typist. On college campuses, they advertise in the school newspapers and on campus bulletin boards. Best of all, type your papers on a word processor or have them typed that way, especially if your teacher expects you to revise them. That way you can make changes and corrections without having to retype the entire paper. Every year, more high schools and colleges offer free student access to

computers and free word-processing classes. Take advantage of these services and save yourself a lot of time and energy.

If you have problems with correct spelling and punctuation, get help with that also. Learn to use the spelling program on a computer. Buy a dictionary and an English handbook. Find a fellow student who is good at proofreading. Hire an editor. Or as a last resort, follow the (humorous) advice of a long-time professor of English and marry someone who can spell. Whatever it takes, don't sabotage your grade by ignoring the standards your teacher sets for the appearance of the paper.

One word of caution. Later, in Chapter 6, I'll advise you to develop an efficient writing process. Part of that advice is the recommendation that you write messy first drafts, concentrating on getting your thoughts down and leaving concerns about spelling and punctuation until you write the second draft. With that in mind, I want to warn you against letting my emphasis on the appearance of the paper hang you up when you're writing. Even if your teacher is a stickler for correctness, you can still forget about it when you write the first draft (for your eyes only), and then be as picky as possible when you go back to look for mistakes. Keep the two steps separate, and you'll do a better job of both.

WAR IS HELL—PARTS OF SPEECH, LOGICAL FALLACIES, AND LITERATURE

Later, I'll discuss research showing that the teaching of grammar is ineffective in improving student writing. So what do you do if your instructors make you learn grammar? Show them the research and ask them to stop teaching grammar? Probably not a good idea. Whether or not you approve of the course content, there's not much hope of your ignoring it without harming your grade (more later about how to deal with grammar).

Your teacher may ask you to memorize the logical fallacies and make sure you don't commit any in your writing. Or you may have to spend an entire semester reading literature and writing critical analyses of short stories, poems, and plays. If you can't find any alternatives to courses whose content you don't like, then my advice is to hold your nose and take the medicine.

Of all the above tips on knowing the enemy and fulfilling requirements, this one could require the most work and cause the greatest amount of frustration. Course content will vary even among teachers who are teaching the same course, and it's simply a fact of life that you won't like some courses or some teachers. So do yourself a favor and look into every possible alternative before you risk an unpleasant experience with a course or teacher you don't like.

CHOOSING YOUR ENEMY

One of the more effective steps you can take to safeguard your GPA from the subjective grading system is to choose your teachers. This won't be easy, especially in high school, and most colleges won't allow you much choice, except for the day and time of the class. But even though it may be difficult, it's still worth a try.

GATHERING INTELLIGENCE FROM ADVANCED SCOUTS

First, talk to as many students as you can who have already taken the course. Find out the grading practices of teachers, and shun the notorious ones. Conversely, the word gets around about which teachers are the fair graders. Also, at many colleges, the student association publishes a manual which lists teachers and describes their practices, based on student reports and even on questionnaires submitted to the teachers themselves. Find out if this kind of manual exists on your campus, and use it when you select possible teachers for your courses.

However, here's a word of caution about well-known, "easy" teachers. Don't let your desire for an A blind you to your true purpose in taking any course, which is to learn something of lasting value. In a recent survey of freshmen who completed English Composition at Pepperdine University, Dr. Lee Ann

Carroll, the Director of Composition, found that students who made A's but felt the course had not challenged them were not as satisfied as others who had made B's yet felt they had worked hard and became better writers. As you will find out in Chapter 6 of this book, writing in school *can* improve your writing and your confidence as a writer, so don't miss out on the opportunity by avoiding courses that require writing or by choosing an easy grader who won't teach you much.

What you want to avoid is any teacher whose grading standards are notoriously arbitrary or unfair. What you're looking for is a fair grader who will give you your money's worth. In fact, when asking other students about teachers, listen for remarks like, "She makes you work, but you learn a lot," or "He's a tough grader, but he's fair." Teachers who combine high expectations with fair grading practices are your best bet.

GATHERING INTELLIGENCE THROUGH THE CLOSE RECONNAISSANCE

After you have narrowed down your list of possible teachers, try your best to interview them. Shop around. Set up appointments with teachers and ask them to read samples of your school writing. Find out what they think about it. Be specific. Ask them what grade they would give your writing. Be ready for them to resist this question. Most teachers frown on what they call the students' "cynical" concern with grades rather than with learning. Still, if you can pressure them for an answer without alienating them, do so. If they are very secretive or defensive about grading, that in itself may be a sign to avoid their courses.

Also in your interview, find out if teachers reward extra effort. If they see you as a B or C writer, ask them what you would have to do to make an A in their course. If they do reward hard work, find out their requirements, and then be willing to meet them.

If you are a first-semester freshman in college, shopping for instructors will be harder but not impossible. You probably know at least one student who has taken freshman English,

and that student knows others. Talk to as many as you can. Or just parachute straight into the enemy's camp and go to the English department or writing program office and ask for the names of all the freshman writing instructors. Interview as many as you can. Do the same for your other courses. Act like a paying customer who wants to see what you are getting before you buy. After all, that's what you are.

If you're a college freshman, another step you can take is to postpone taking freshman English for a semester. Then, you can take the above steps much more easily. You can talk to fellow freshmen while they are taking the course, find out their teachers' grading practices, read their course descriptions, and go through the interview steps during teachers' scheduled office hours.

Once again, be prepared for a system that is set up to keep you from putting off college English for a semester, but keep it in mind as one of the better alternatives for more than one reason. Oddly enough, students who wait to take freshman English tend to do better than first-semester freshmen. Perhaps the writing practice you get in other college courses prepares you better for college English. I know that sounds backward. Freshman English is supposed to prepare you to write better in college. But if taking on the system in reverse order works for you, don't knock it.

You can use this method of interviewing teachers for any course that requires writing for a grade. In fact, all these pre-course interview techniques will gain in effectiveness the further along you progress in your college career and the more freedom you are allowed in selecting your courses. So even if you don't get to choose your teacher for freshman English, try these methods when selecting other courses that include writing as part of the course requirements.

I know this sounds like a lot of trouble to go through before you even set foot in class. I also realize that the idea of interviewing teachers may scare you, especially if you are a freshman in college. I don't blame you if you feel wary of the prospect of grilling prospective teachers about their courses and their reactions to your writing. So if this seems too much to ask, don't do it, and don't feel guilty about passing up this option. Instead, place your major efforts into the methods designed to help you once you're in a class. But regardless of whether or not you are willing or able to choose your teacher, you're now ready to apply what you've learned to do once you have enrolled in a class.

PRIDE AND PREJUDICE IN DECEIVING THE ENEMY

As I look back over the lessons in this chapter, I see places where I appear to ask you to curry favor with your teachers, to perform the role of a model student just to improve your grade, even to deceive your teachers by acting as if you are interested in a course that is boring you to the point of brain death. Is that what I am asking you to do? Is it? No, not at all.

By taking the actions I suggest, you may actually become more interested in your courses, finding unexpected resources in the course materials and surprising support from your teachers. But even if you don't experience such pleasant outcomes, you can look at this as performing a balancing act between your pride and the teacher's prejudice.

Throughout the book, I talk about teacher bias and the effect it has on your grade. I also talk about your ability to influence the bias in your favor. Some of this may run counter to your moral code. I know that some people cannot follow Mickey Mouse rules without putting up a fight. They even enjoy venting their frustration on the teacher, digging in their heels over the petty requirements of punctuality and classroom behavior, or the picky concern with correctness and grammar. If you feel honor-bound to react that way, it's all right. You have to do what you have to do to feel right about your actions. Just be aware that in acting that way, you can determine a significant part of your grade before you hand in your first paper.

Remember the research that showed the effect of stamping "honors" on a paper? Well, look at it this way. Through all the actions discussed in this chapter, you can stamp a message on your papers. It could be something like, "Your course is worthless." On the other hand, it could be, "I am doing my best to fulfill your requirements." In other words, through the methods described above, you can stamp "honors" on your papers even before you hand them in. And the beauty of most of these techniques is that they don't require extra work, just the avoidance of self-defeating behaviors like being late or talking in class.

If I were to summarize the message that runs through this chapter, it might be similar to the cynical advice traditionally given to recruits: "Keep your eyes and ears open, your mouth shut, and don't volunteer for nothin'." But since I am not a cynic, and you are not a recruit, I'll modify it somewhat to: "Keep your eyes and ears open, your mouth shut while the teacher is talking, and save your volunteering for where it counts the most." Where is that? That's what the next chapter will tell you.

5

WHAT IF THEY GAVE A WAR AND NO ONE CAME? HOW TO REACT TO YOUR FIRST GRADED PAPER

To fight and conquer in all your battles is not supreme excellence; supreme excellence consists in breaking the enemy's resistance without fighting.

Sun Tzu
The Art of War

The previous chapter dealt with what you can do to ensure a high grade even before you turn in any writing. This chapter will show you what to do after you have written your first paper and received it back with a grade you don't like. In the next chapter, I'll tell you how to improve your grade by improving your writing. This may seem a bit out of order. Shouldn't I tell you how to write a better paper *before* I tell you what to do after you get it back? Not really.

Why? Because the methods in the next chapter take time to apply, whereas almost all those in this chapter will help you become a more effective student simply by reading about them. Once again, some of these methods won't require any extra work, just extra smarts, and some of them will require you to work harder. But of all the chapters in the book, this one contains the greatest promise of helping you raise your grade the most in the short space of one semester, without generating conflict with your teacher.

HIT 'EM WHERE THEY AIN'T

Imagine that the first shot has now been fired. You turned in a paper, and the teacher gave it back, perhaps "soaked in red," maybe just slashed with a low grade and a few nasty comments. What do you do now? The first lesson concerns what *not* to do. It requires you to follow the rule of warfare that warns against attacking your enemies at their point of greatest strength. Instead, you're supposed to "hit 'em where they ain't," the point at which they least expect your attack.

All teachers have grown to expect students' complaints about almost any grade other than an A (yes, even an A–); thus, they are well fortified to resist. So, you simply don't complain

about your grade. There are several ways to change your teacher's bias toward your writing, but arguing about the grade isn't one of them.

OK. If complaining about the specific grade on your paper won't help, how about taking this book to your teachers and showing them the research on grading? Then maybe you could get them to change their entire system. Again, this is not a very good idea. Remember the 151 new teachers of freshman English who took the grading seminars at USC? Even though they learned firsthand how subjective their *own* grading could be, and even though the program at USC allowed instructors to use a modified system involving grading of fewer papers, as far as I know, not many of the new teachers gave up the practice of grading every one of their own students' papers. As another reminder of the effects of this grading system, I offer the following from Dr. Paul Diederich, author of the research we examined earlier:

> Bias appears most obviously when a teacher is grading the papers of his own students, knowing who wrote them. If a teacher reads the paper of a boy known to be dull, careless, and impertinent, it would take a remarkable paper to overcome the prejudice that the teacher has formed against him. On the other hand, if the paper was written by a model student, or by one with whom the teacher sympathizes because he has recently had serious trouble at home, the grade is likely to be higher than a dispassionate analysis of the writing would warrant.
>
> Even when the paper of a given student surprises or disappoints us, we are likely to change too little. When I get a poor paper from a good student who generally writes well, I tend to think, "Too bad; he had an off day. I'm afraid that I'll have to lower his grade to a B." But if that same paper had been written by a poor student, it could easily get a D or an F. (*Measuring Growth in English,* page 11)

If Diederich himself recognizes the entrenched, rigid quality of bias in his own grading, how much more rigidly will teachers defend their grading practice when they don't share Diederich's experience and knowledge about the subjectivity of the system? I can see a bloody battle to the death; the death, that is, of your GPA. To avoid that kind of battle, this chapter will teach you further lessons in guerrilla warfare, in giving ground, in dodging your teacher's bullets. Your effort will be to fight a secret war to end all wars, so that your teachers will never even know a war is being fought.

The focal point of your attack is your teacher's perception of your writing. From what you have learned so far in this chapter, you know your goal is to change your teacher's perception without arguing about your grade or your teacher's grading system. What can you do instead? Your alternatives fall under two main categories.

First, there are methods you can use to improve your writing. That's supposedly the purpose of freshman writing in the first place, and in the next chapter, I'll tell you how you can do that in the most effective way. The only problem is, the teacher may not perceive the improvement. Remember what Diederich said about teacher bias and how unchanging it tends to be once it is formed.

But there's another message in Diederich's statements that points us toward the second category of alternatives. Diederich claims that once teachers see you as a model student, their bias toward your writing is influenced in your favor. In the last chapter, we discussed techniques that can establish you as a model student *before* your teacher sees your writing. In the remainder of this chapter, we will look at ways to create a model impression even after the teacher has graded your writing down. What this means is that you can use your teachers' perception of you as a *student* to pull up their perception of your writing.

THE PEACE CONFERENCE

All right. You're in a class where your teacher doesn't think very much of your writing. Your goal now is to establish yourself as a person who is willing to work to improve. The best way to do this is in private, individual conferences with the teacher. All college instructors are required to hold "office hours," regularly scheduled times they are available to meet with students. Once again, follow Sun Tzu's advice: "If the enemy leaves a door open, you must rush in." Find out your teacher's hours and make an appointment to work on your paper. When I say work, I mean it. As I warned you before, this is not a time to harangue your teacher about the grade on the paper. Focus your remarks on your intention to improve your writing, and the grade will take care of itself.

Take a photocopy of the paper with the instructor's marks and comments, and tell your instructor you want to find out what to do to revise it. While your instructor is discussing the paper, take notes on your copy, and ask questions to make sure you know exactly what the teacher wants. If you're not sure about a suggestion for improvement, ask for an example. Get your instructor to tell you what he or she would have written or added or deleted in that particular spot. Then write down what your instructor says.

Also, ask your instructor for sample papers that illustrate better writing, especially papers written for the same assignment. If he or she has none, find out which of your classmates wrote the best papers and ask them to let you read their work. This way, you'll get a feel for your instructor's idea of good writing. Then, actually revise your paper and ask your teacher to comment on it again in conference.

If possible, see if your teacher will let you rewrite for a higher grade, but even if he or she won't change the grade, revise the paper and set up another conference. If your teacher is still critical of your paper, don't be discouraged. Every bit of work and every conference will pay off in two ways. First, whether or not you improve your writing on any "absolute" scale, you will change your papers in the way the teacher wants. This will change the teacher's perception of the quality of your writing, thus raising your grade. And second, your teacher will obviously take note of the extra work you are putting into the course. In a society like ours, which respects effort, especially extra effort, the chances are good that the teacher will raise your grade for the effort alone, even if he or she doesn't think your writing has improved. (Where do you think the expression, "A for effort," came from?)

You may think that these strategies won't work with *your* teachers, but you'll never know unless you try them. Karina, our guerrilla writer, set up writing conferences with every professor she had at Pepperdine, and she reports from the "enemy" camp that they all made helpful suggestions for improving her papers and showed her sample A papers from previous classes.

Karina claims that, instead of becoming cynical about the subjectivity of professors' grades, she developed a strong awareness of writing to a specific audience, and this awareness has benefited her legal writing as well as the writing she did in school.

So, take your papers to conference, revise them, and take them to conference again. Do this with every paper, if need be, and your work will pay off.

A SECRET WEAPON: THE WRITING CENTER

One of the best-kept secrets on college campuses is how much a writing center can help you raise your writing grade. If your school has one, use it. It will help in two major ways. First, taking a paper in any stage of writing and getting help from an instructor will result in a more well-thought-out and well-written paper and a higher grade. And the second benefit will come when you let your teacher know you are putting in the extra time and effort on your papers.

However, let me give you one word of warning. Your experience with any writing center will depend on which instructor you happen to choose. If you don't have a good first experience, don't give up. Try other instructors until you find one who works well with you. Then make appointments with that specific instructor. Better still, find two writing center intructors who work well with you so that you won't ever be caught with a paper due when your favorite instructor already has an appointment. Then you'll always have one in reserve—sound tactics in writing as well as war.

And one additional word of warning. Sometimes a writing center tutor may help you revise your paper extensively, and yet it still won't please your classroom instructor. Remember Karina's experience with the Pepperdine Writing Center and her freshman seminar teacher? Sometimes the person who helps you with a paper may like it just fine, but your teacher won't like it at all. Other times, they may agree. This outcome is not so surprising given what we know about the different grades a paper will receive from different teachers. Also, it underscores my earlier advice to take your papers to your instructors for conferences. The writing center can help in many ways, but ultimately, the standards you have to meet in any course are those of the person who decides your grade.

To lend additional strength to my point, I offer this final example. One summer session when I was teaching in USC's writing center, a student brought in the second paper he had to write for a literature class. He was worried about the course for several reasons. First, he had received a D– on his first paper (along with some insulting comments from the teacher), and he didn't have any confidence that he could do better on this paper. Even worse, this course was the last he had to take in order to graduate that summer. He didn't like literature courses, but he had waited to finish off one general education requirement. This was the only course offered that summer that fulfilled it, so he couldn't drop the course and still get his degree.

After I gave him specific advice on writing his paper, I recommended the plan I have outlined above, essentially that he take each paper to a conference with his teacher, and rewrite each one according to his teacher's instructions. I didn't see him again until near the end of the summer session, when I ran into him on campus and asked him how he was doing in class.

He said he was following the plan and conferencing with the instructor with every paper. He was now getting B's on his papers, and he was sure to get at least a C+ in the course, which was fine with him since the grade didn't affect his plans after graduation.

Once again, the lesson of both cases is to get help from your writing center, but your best resource for revision is the person who grades your paper.

WHEN ALL ELSE FAILS— ALLIES IN THE ENEMY CAMP

What happens if you try everything I recommended so far, and your teacher still gives you low grades on your writing? My advice is that you drop the course and try again with another instructor. In high school, this option may not exist, but almost all colleges allow students to drop courses during a specified period of time with no penalty to their grade point average. The period varies from school to school, but it usually extends through two-thirds of the semester or quarter.

Before the deadline, you will have gotten a good idea of what your final grade is going to be. If you aren't certain, ask your instructor. If he or she is evasive, tell him or her why you want to know, and if you still don't get an answer, make an appeal to the department (I'll tell you how in a minute) or drop the course.

Even though instructors may claim to have good reasons for withholding your grade, they don't outweigh your right to know. In fact, at many colleges, instructors are required to let you know your grade at midterm, and some schools even require teachers to inform students in writing when they are in danger of failing the course, at any point during the semester when that becomes the case.

Of course there will be disadvantages to dropping the course. First of all, you will have to take it again, but if you complete the course with a failing grade, you will have to retake it anyway, and then the F will lower your GPA. In some schools, you have to repeat the course, even if you make a D. The most difficult decisions involve whether or not to drop a course in which you're making a C or B in order to try for an even higher grade. Add to this dilemma the fact that you'll have to pay to take the course again, and at some schools, the cost can be considerable.

So let me give you two options short of dropping the course, both involving the appeals process. First, while you're still taking the course, some schools allow you to lodge a complaint or appeal if you believe you are receiving unfair treatment. Find out about this possibility from your advisor or from the writing program office. At USC, for example, you can talk to an administrator of the Freshman Writing Program who will read your papers and consult with your instructor if something seems amiss.

The same appeals process applies to students who have finished the course and feel they were graded unfairly. It is essential in both these situations that you save all your papers and the instructor's comments, as they constitute the only evidence you have to make your case. Especially if you rewrote papers for the teacher and went to the writing center for additional help, save copies of papers and revisions, and keep some sort of record of your work in the writing center.

A few semesters ago, I had a student who was repeating the course with me because she made a D the first time she took it with another teacher. When talking about her first experience, she said she had rewritten papers for the teacher and made several visits to the writing center. She had expected to pass, and in fact had no indication otherwise until she received her grade report in the mail during Christmas break.

When she returned to campus, she went and asked her former teacher why she had failed after putting in so much extra work. The instructor answered that the student had only put in the "appearance of extra work." Of course, my student wonders why her teacher didn't tell her this during the semester, when she still had a chance to drop the course.

In this case, I haven't heard the teacher's side of the story, but if it did happen as my student tells me, then it represents the worst outcome for you as a student. You work hard all semester, believing your efforts will be rewarded, yet your teacher fails you without advanced warning. The only course open to you is the appeals process discussed above, and it can be a powerful tool. Remember, teachers are only human. We too can fall prey to human weakness and commit acts of negligence, malice, and malpractice, just like doctors, lawyers, stockbrokers, and plumbers. So always save copies of your papers and don't be afraid to take the necessary steps to protect your interests.

Now, one last word about what to do if you decide to drop the course. Don't just wait around until next semester and trust your luck to give you a teacher who likes your writing. Go through the steps of talking to students who are taking the course and interviewing prospective instructors. Find one who likes your writing and/or will reward extra effort with a higher grade. If this takes a couple of semesters, it's OK. Just take it easy and do a good job of finding the right instructor. You have nothing to lose except the pain of struggling through another semester with the wrong one.

FIGHT THIS WAR WITH YOUR OWN WEAPONS: DON'T PLAGIARIZE

At this point, I've covered the major lessons of fighting a clandestine war against your teacher's perception of your writing. But there's one lesson I've saved for the last section of this chapter, because I want it to stick in your memory. I can sum it up in two words: DON'T PLAGIARIZE! Don't ever give in to the temptation to hand in someone else's writing as your own. I know the temptation exists, and it can come in many forms.

For example, you might be taking a course from the same instructor who taught a friend of yours last semester and who is assigning several of the same essay topics. Your friend made A's on these assignments, and he or she suggests you might want to use the A papers. Why not change them a little here and there and turn them in as your own?

Or, here's another case. What if you find a magazine article or a newspaper editorial that fits an assignment? Why not just use it or change it slightly to make it fit better? Finally, how about those term-paper services that advertise on college campuses? Why not save yourself a lot of time and just buy a term paper?

I know how strong the pressure is to make a good grade, especially with so much of your future riding on your GPA.

Without that pressure, you wouldn't be reading this book. Also, what is so immoral about paying someone to write a paper when our top leaders in government pay professionals to write their speeches, and corporations pay ad agencies to create commercials in which actors are paid to play the parts of satisfied customers?

The line between right and wrong can often be hard to find, but look at it this way. Even if the morality of turning in others' work doesn't bother you, consider the practical aspects. What happens if you get caught? You could fail the course, be suspended from school, or even expelled for good. You may think the chances are in your favor, but consider the following examples.

Several years ago, two of my students turned in identical papers that they must have copied from the same magazine article. Imagine their surprise when I showed each the other's paper. Even though the chances of this happening to you are small, it happens.

How about the chances of getting by with using a friend's work? OK, let's see. Recently, a fellow instructor told me about a student who had written some excellent papers out of class, but when he had to write in-class essays, the level of his writing dropped drastically. The instructor became suspicious, so he scheduled a conference with the student and quizzed him on the content of the papers the student had "written" out of class. The student couldn't answer any of the questions that required knowledge of his *own* papers. Result: The instructor started administrative proceedings accusing the student of plagiarism.

The saddest example I know involving a student's use of a friend's work happened in another fellow instructor's class. The instructor had assigned a combination paper/oral presentation, and as one student was reading hers to the class, the instructor recognized part of the material as the work of a well-known writer in the field of literary criticism. When the instructor confronted the student after class, she burst into tears and said she wasn't responsible for plagiarizing the author.

"How could that be?" the instructor asked.

"Because my boyfriend wrote the speech for me," the student said angrily, "and he didn't tell me he had plagiarized."

The most dangerous situation of all involves the term paper. Teachers look very closely at "research" papers of any sort to make sure you document material properly and indicate what material is directly quoted. Thus, they are very likely to spot bought or borrowed material, since they are looking especially hard for work that's not your own.

Just recently, a fellow instructor told me she read a student paper that she felt was written by a professional service. So, at the next class meeting, she announced to her students that someone in the class had turned in a bought paper. She expressed her disappointment and said she was going to cancel class that day and wanted to talk to the guilty person immediately in her office. Then she left the classroom and walked straight to her office. After she unlocked the door and put her books on the desk, she turned to see half a dozen of her students in the hallway, waiting in line to talk to her!

So my message remains: Don't copy, don't borrow, don't buy, don't lie. Do your own work.

I realize my warnings may actually have an effect that's the opposite of what I intend. Some students may take them as a challenge and decide to show me that they can fool their instructors with work that's not their own. And, after all, doesn't everyone know someone who has gotten away with it? Nothing I could say here will stop that kind of person from plagiarizing. However, by this point, I have discussed numerous ways to earn your A that don't risk failure or expulsion yet do allow you to act with integrity. I will discuss additional methods for raising your grade in the following chapters. Stick with these methods, and you won't ever need to take the risks involved in plagiarizing.

6

• •

STAR WARS: RESEARCH ON THE BEST WEAPONS IN THE WARS OF WRITING

• •

What enables the wise sovereign and the good general to strike and conquer, and achieve things beyond the reach of ordinary men [and women] is foreknowledge.

Sun Tzu
The Art of War

In the best of all possible worlds, to improve the grade your writing receives, you would simply improve your writing. But we've seen how a teacher's subjective perception of your writing can prevent such a commonsense outcome, and I have suggested that you direct your major efforts toward changing the teacher's perception of your writing, whether or not you change the quality of the writing itself. In fact, given the flawed system of grading, it may seem that it makes no sense to talk of writing quality or improvement.

If teachers aren't likely to see the improvement in your writing, and if the quality of writing can't be measured with validity, why waste a chapter telling you how to improve it? Good question, and the answer comes in several parts.

It turns out that writing quality can be measured with validity, that you can improve the quality of your writing, and that the improvement can be measured. Thus it makes sense to improve your writing to get a higher grade. But doesn't this contradict what we learned earlier from research? No, and here's why.

The research we looked at examines what happens when individual teachers grade papers. The goal of the research was to find a more valid means of grading essays, and that goal was reached. It involved using two graders instead of one and even a third when the first two grades differed widely. Diederich and his associates applied the system in school settings and found they could measure improvement in writing over the course of a year. Also, similar grading techniques allow researchers to study different methods of teaching writing to see which have the greatest effect on improving the quality of student writing.

"OK," you're saying, "this sounds like good news for anyone in a school that uses this grading system. But how does it help me if my school doesn't use it?" Another good question.

First, it means that you can improve your writing even before you take a course, so that you can improve your chances of getting a higher initial grade from any instructor, and start out at a higher level in your teacher's perception.

What does it do for you if you are already in a class and receiving low grades on your writing? Not much, unless you utilize the methods for changing your teacher's perception of you as a student. Then, the combination can result in your teacher's seeing and rewarding the improvement as well as your willingness to work. The result: an A in the course.

In addition to improving your grade, there are other reasons to improve your writing, and they concern the true purposes of any writing course. And what might they be?

Three major areas of improvement come to mind. First, improved writing skills—you will learn specific strategies for any type of writing task. Second, greater confidence in your writing—you will feel more able to handle writing assignments in school and beyond. And third, a reduced aversion to writing—you will learn how to make the act of writing easier, less painful, and even a pleasure.

Unfortunately, with all the pressure and worry that go along with most writing courses, you rarely finish them with the feeling you have accomplished these goals. Yet such outcomes are possible. You can improve your writing skills, your confidence in your writing, and the ease with which you write. And even though these gains may or may not improve your grade in English 101 this semester, they will make the experience of writing your way through it more bearable.

So, for all the above reasons, I include this chapter and the next. The methods discussed are based on research on the composing process, the teaching of writing, and on writing apprehension and writing block. I include enough alternatives so you can find something that works in just about any area in which you now feel a lack.

WRITING WEAPONS: THE STATE OF THE ART

In spite of the impression many teachers will give you, we are only recently gaining any degree of certainty about what works best in improving writing. Of course we are certain about the correct spelling of words and correct punctuation. In other words, the rules of written English are set down in rule books and can be taught. In fact, in too many English classes, this is about all that gets taught and then enforced by the teacher's red marks and grades on your papers. But teaching writing as a set of rules is like teaching karate with a handbook of written directions. And though there is some agreement about the best way to learn a sport, there is considerable controversy among teachers about the best way to learn to write. Happily, there's a growing body of knowledge that points toward some directions (some new and surprising), and steers us away from others (also unexpected).

Reviews of research on the composing process and the teaching of writing indicate several "do's and don'ts." First, in order to write better, you need to read more, especially the kind of writing you plan to improve upon (more specifics in a minute). Second, you need to write more of that kind of writing, but not as much as you might expect. Third, practice "sentence combining" (I'll tell you how). Fourth, keep a "free-writing" journal. Fifth, develop an efficient writing process. And finally, beware of critics bearing red pens. That's basically it.

"That simple?" you may ask.

"That simple," I answer, but simple doesn't mean easy or quick. As Sun Tzu says, "One may know how to conquer without being able to do it." Improving your writing is simple in the sense that improving your tennis game is simple. All you need to do is watch as many pro matches as you can, play tennis yourself, and find a tennis instructor who doesn't spend most of the lesson pointing out what you did wrong, who "shows" more than "tells." Simple. Yet how quickly would your tennis game improve? Well, your writing may not improve that quickly. But be patient and take the following steps, all of which you can do on your own, without a teacher's help. Research indicates that with persistence and time, your efforts will pay off.

WRITING POWER GROWS FROM THE PAGES OF A BOOK (OR THE SIDES OF A CEREAL BOX)

Above, I said to read more of the type of writing that you want to improve. For most high school and college courses, that means nonfiction prose, in other words, newspapers, magazines, and books with factual subjects. Don't think this means you have to read serious, boring writing in order to improve. In fact, the opposite may be the case. In research at USC, Professor Stephen Krashen found a significant correlation between high scores on writing and the amount of *pleasure* reading students had done outside of school. So the more you enjoy your reading, the chances are the more you'll do, thereby developing the "feel" for good writing that comes with increased reading.

Your reading program can include articles from any section of the newspaper (sports, fashion, editorial), from magazine articles on any subject that interests you (movie stars,

computers, surfing), and from books with subjects that grab your attention and keep you reading (the sinking of the *Titanic*, how to find a job, the secret world of the CIA)—just so the writing describes, explains, argues a point, or tells you how to do something.

To prepare specifically for writing papers in composition classes, read as much student writing as you can. Ask your friends in high school or college classes to let you read their papers (preferably A papers, but we know the grade is relative to the teacher), and read the assignments that generated the papers. Also, read as many different papers as you can on the same assignment so that you can see the variety of ways you can approach any writing task.

For some very good examples of college writing, get a copy of *The Bedford Prizes: Student Writers at Work*. The prize-winning essays in this book were first written in college classes to fulfill writing assignments, so at one and the same time, you get a picture of the best student writing and the kind of assignments to expect in college.

TRAIN WITH YOUR WEAPONS, DON'T STRAIN

In addition to reading the type of writing you want to improve, you need to write that kind of writing. Once again, that means nonfiction prose. Several studies indicate that the largest gains in writing improvement are made when students are taught strategies for recalling information and transforming it to write their own nonfiction essays. The recall strategies include techniques such as listing ideas, brainstorming, and clustering (see the Bibliography under Hillocks). You can find out how to use these strategies in Appendix C, "A Guerrilla Writer's Handbook."

The type of nonfiction writing you need to practice could be as simple as observing an object and describing in writing what you see, or as complex as choosing a controversial issue and constructing an argument that you support with facts.

If that definition sounds familiar, it should. It's the kind of writing you find in newspapers, magazines, and books with factual subjects. First, I suggested that you read it; then I said you need to write it. I also said you may not need to write as much as you might expect. On this point, research indicates that a combination of reading and writing is just as effective in improving writing as increasing the frequency of writing. In one study cited by Professor Krashen of USC, college freshmen who wrote twenty-four essays in one semester experienced no more improvement than freshmen who wrote only eight essays and read nonfiction selections from a reader (see the Bibliography under Krashen).

Of course, that's good news for those of you who dislike writing, but it doesn't tell us exactly how much you need to write in order to improve. So, as a rule of thumb, try writing a practice paper every other week, using some of the sample assignments in Appendix B of this book. Or you could write the assignments that generate the papers you get from friends. Then you'll gain the additional advantage of experimenting with strategies your friends used in writing their papers as well as having papers to compare to your own.

CONCENTRATING YOUR FORCES

The third method I recommended for improving your writing was sentence combining. Research indicates that practicing these exercises improves the quality of student writing, and you don't need to take a class to learn how to do them (see the Bibliography under Hillocks). Just get a copy of any book that contains the exercises. I recommend William Strong's *Sentence Combining: A Composing Book,* because it takes you through the exercises without any unnecessary terminology.

However, if you don't have the desire or initiative to do this on your own, don't worry too much about it. Through your reading, you'll attain the same goal, which is to increase your supply of alternatives in sentence structure and style. You just won't improve as quickly as you would if you practiced the exercises.

A HEALTHY WRITER IS A HAPPY WARRIOR

Next, I suggested you keep a "free-writing" journal. This simply involves nonstop writing for a certain amount of time every day on anything that comes to mind. It could be as little as ten minutes and consist of an unrestrained, uncensored, stream-of-consciousness story. The purpose is to free your ideas and increase your willingness to write without worrying about the quality of the writing. With practice, this can reduce the inhibitions you may now feel when faced with a blank page and the necessity to write. (Directions for free writing are contained in Appendix C, "A Guerrilla Writer's Handbook.")

An additional advantage of keeping this kind of journal is that it can help you feel better, physically and emotionally. Research at Southern Methodist University by Dr. James Pennebaker indicates that adults who wrote about their problems made gains over those who wrote about superficial topics (see the Bibliography). These gains were measured in three ways. First, post-study blood tests showed improved immune systems in the group members who wrote about their problems, but not in the group that wrote about superficial topics. Second, follow-up tests given six weeks after both groups stopped writing found that the problem-writing group's advantage still held. And third, both six-week and six-month comparisons between the frequency of doctor visits of the two groups found the problem-writing group to be healthier. The researchers also found that the healthiest of all the writers were those who wrote about their problems *and* the feelings the problems generated. Given the strength of these results, maybe the biggest surprise is that they were produced by only five days of writing!

The lesson for you is that you can write about your problems and the way you feel about them, and at one and the same time, benefit your writing and your health.

WRITING SMARTER, NOT HARDER

Some of our problems with writing stem from an overemphasis in school on the finished product. Students are assigned the published works of professional writers and asked to write similar pieces. When students try to fulfill such assignments, their own efforts seem to fall so far short of those written by professionals, they often give up in frustration. No one tells the students that the published works are the results of several efforts by the writers, a process during which the first draft may bear little resemblance to the finished product.

Well, I'm here to tell you, and also to assure you that, if writing is a struggle, it doesn't mean you can't write. In fact, you can learn to make writing less of a struggle, and we'll take a look at research on the composing processes of good and poor writers to find out how.

Krashen found that good writers plan more before they begin writing—not necessarily a formal plan like the Roman numeral outlines many of us were forced to write, but some kind of rough plan, in thought or on paper. Then, once they begin writing, good writers stop more often and reread what they have written, an act that keeps them aware of where they have been and where they need to go.

When good writers revise, they make more changes in the content of what they have written rather than changes for correctness. Then, after they are fairly satisfied with the ideas they have communicated, they edit for correctness. Also, good writers are more willing to return to earlier phases of the process, like planning, whenever they think of new ideas or when new information becomes available. In other words, they remain open to changing their ideas even after they have committed them to paper.

Research also indicates that some student writers may make writing easier if they first write down their ideas without worrying about the audience and then rewrite with the audience in mind. As with many complex acts, it may help to take one step at a time.

For specific methods to help develop a more efficient writing process, see Appendix C, "A Guerrilla Writer's Handbook." However, keep in mind that there's no such thing as *the* correct writing process. For example, I've had good writers in my classes who did all their pre-planning mentally, others who wrote rough notes, and still others who created formal outlines, complete with Roman numerals. You may already know that your way of getting your ideas on paper works fine for you. Or you may be dissatisfied with some aspect of your process and want to experiment with some of the methods in Appendix C to see if they help you generate ideas and write them with greater ease.

Regardless of what you decide to do in relation to improving your writing process, keep in mind the principal message of this section: Most of us can benefit from taking a looser approach to our first drafts, concentrating more on *what* we want to say than *how* we want to say it.

BEWARE OF CRITICS BEARING RED PENS

My final recommendation for improving your writing was that you beware of giving your writing to red-marking teachers, and I include in this category your overly critical friends or fellow students. I can hear many of you asking how you'll ever know what to improve if you don't know what you have done wrong. Intuitively, this seems to be a valid question, and after all, this has been your experience in school. Your teachers red-marked all your errors and expected you to correct them.

However, of all the methods examined in research on teaching composition, the intensive correction of errors was the only one that actually resulted in a negative effect on the quality of student writing (see the Bibliography under Hillocks). In other words, correcting every error creates the opposite effect of what teachers intend, maybe because students are overwhelmed by all the negative feedback, and they give up hope of ever being able to get it all right. So they also give up writing. Whatever the reasons, research has measured the negative effects of the practice, so stay away from having your writing corrected intensively.

What do you do, then, about mistakes? You can follow the advice I mentioned earlier: "If you are one of those who can't spell, try to marry someone who can" (see the Bibliography under Wilson). If you have such awful problems with spelling and punctuation that you can't correct your own drafts with the help of a dictionary or handbook, find a friend who will edit your writing without reacting in a judgmental fashion. You may also get help at the writing center, although some centers won't proofread for every mistake. Finally, you might learn how to avoid the most common errors college students make by reading *Under the Grammar Hammer: The 25 Most Important Grammar Mistakes and How to Avoid Them*. It was written by none other than your own Chairman, Douglas Cazort, and with all the modesty I can muster, I can heartily recommend it for those of you who suffer from fear of grammar and spelling.

Whatever you do about errors, don't let the concern for correctness come between you and your most important purpose in writing, which is to say what you want to say. If an overconcern for correctness and style already inhibits your writing, then the most important steps you can take involve the recommendations from the previous section on improving your writing process: Make a rough plan before you write. Then write rough drafts for your eyes only—messy drafts with plenty of mistakes and plenty of ideas. Then go back later to revise, adding or subtracting material, working on the way you said things, and directing your writing to a specific audience. Finally, edit for spelling and punctuation or have an editor/ friend edit for you. Separating the emphasis on meaning and correctness will help you do a better job of both.

YOUR FUTURE AS A WRITING WARRIOR

That's about it for the most effective methods of improving your writing, and along with it, your grades. It may seem like a lot when it's looked at all at once, but taken one step at a time, it doesn't have to be painful. Read the types of nonfiction you enjoy. Practice writing it. Keep a journal of "free writing" about your problems and feelings. Separate writing from editing. And protect your writing from negative judges.

Then, once you're free of required writing courses, maybe, just maybe, you'll find other reasons to write. Now you'll know how to get better at it and even how to enjoy it more. Whatever your future relation to writing, you have the basic knowledge required to grow as a writer, without a teacher or even in spite of one.

7

DEFEATING THE ENEMY WITHIN: BREAKING THROUGH WRITING ANXIETY AND WRITING BLOCK

A whole army may be robbed of its spirit; a
commander in chief may be robbed of his
presence of mind.

Sun Tzu
The Art of War

Valerie, a freshman English student, sits at a desk in her
dorm room staring at a blank sheet of paper. She
thinks of one sentence after another but rejects each
in turn as not being good enough. Several teachers in
her past have told her how important it is to write a good
introduction, one that will grab the reader's attention. Also, her
freshman English teacher instructed the class not to turn in
any papers that aren't interesting. He said he doesn't want to
spend the semester being bored by student papers.

As far as Valerie is concerned, nothing she writes can meet
these standards, so she will spend two more hours rejecting her

efforts to write a perfect, interesting introduction. With time running out, she will finally squeeze out a beginning she doesn't like and then rush painfully through the remainder of the paper.

Dave is a good writer and knows it, yet he doesn't enjoy writing. He hates every new assignment because he feels he has to match or beat his last performance. When the pressure is strongest, he finds writing almost impossible, and his grades in writing class reflect his difficulty.

Sarah sits in class, writing an essay exam. Recently, her teacher told her not to use so many simple sentences in her papers. Today in her essay, Sarah tries to write complex sentences but finds it hard to think about the answer to the question and her sentence style at the same time. When the hour is up, Sarah knows already that her essay doesn't fully answer the question. As she hands in her paper, she feels a pang of dread thinking of the grade it will receive.

Matt begins a sentence and stops in the middle to look up the spelling of a word. When he tries to finish the sentence, he

realizes he has lost his train of thought while searching through the dictionary.

I could keep on listing examples of writers, each with a different problem that makes writing a painful task. Research is full of case studies of a variety of problems, and I have met a number of students in my classes, some of whose problems are the opposite of others' (one student can't start her papers, another can't finish his). But what do all these problems have to do with making an A in courses that require writing?

I'm glad you asked.

First, research on writing apprehension and writing block has shown a significant, negative correlation between levels of students' writing apprehension and the grades they receive on essay exams. In other words, students who score high on tests of writing apprehension or writing block tend to make low grades on their writing. Keep in mind that even though a negative correlation exists between the two, this doesn't mean that writing apprehension causes low grades. It only means that the two exist together in an inverse relationship (the higher the one, the lower the other). But without any clear indication of a third factor that causes both, their present relation gives you a reasonable motivation to try to lower your writing apprehension in order to raise the grades your writing receives. That's the first reason for this chapter's existence.

The second reason is that even if the process of reducing writing apprehension and blocks didn't raise your grade, it would still be worth the trouble. As you can see from the above student examples, writing can be a painful, time-consuming experience. If as many as 80 percent of students avoid courses, majors, or careers that require writing, then anything we can do to reduce the pain and conflict involved could affect us in life-changing ways. So, let's get on with it.

WE HAVE MET THE ENEMY, AND IT IS US

Even though writing problems come in a wide variety, all of them share one characteristic: the experience of emotional conflict. At the heart of any form of painful writing, there is a battle between one emotion and another, usually triggered by conflicting ideas. These conflicts can range from the mild to the extreme, from a thought that causes you very little concern to one that brings on heart-pounding fear. Also, the ease with which you can resolve these conflicts usually varies according to their intensity.

For example, you might have learned a punctuation rule that requires you to use commas to separate three or more items in a series, but you're not sure whether to place a comma before the conjunction. This uncertainty probably wouldn't cause you much concern, because you know you can easily find the answer in a handbook.

However, a problem that can cause greater conflict involves the so-called "five-paragraph" theme. Many students have learned that a "good" paper will have an introductory paragraph, three "main-body" paragraphs (each of which develops a separate idea), and a concluding paragraph. Quite often, students who have learned this format will experience strong conflict when they think of less than three main ideas to develop in the body paragraphs, and even when they think of more than three. Still, when an instructor tells these students that an essay can contain as many major ideas (and paragraphs) as necessary to get the point across, or as few, most students will relinquish the old format and write with less worry.

The worst conflicts arise when students perceive the threat of failure as a consequence of their writing. This can happen in response to a number of situations. For example, a teacher may state requirements that can lead to failure ("Make two mistakes, and your paper gets an F!"). Or students may react to an internalized standard that they feel they can't meet ("Your introduction must capture the reader's attention!"). Or the thought that a teacher will read and grade a paper can trigger such anxiety in some students that they can't even begin to write. Some of these students may need to seek counseling to resolve their conflicts; others may only need to find different teachers; still others will be able to make do with the techniques in this book.

Which brings me to a problem of my own. Faced with the variety of writing problems and the range of conflicts involved, what can I do to help? Specifically, how do I equip you to help yourself when I don't know your individual problem? Well, I can't, at least not in the way I would if I dealt with you as an individual student sitting in my office.

Still, as we have already learned, we aren't dealing with the best of all possible worlds. We can get by with imperfection, with what works best given the situation. And in the case of reducing the pain of writing, research indicates that some methods work for a wide variety of problems, from the writer who cannot start writing to the one who cannot finish.

From these methods, I have chosen two that research has shown to be the most effective in reducing the conflicts of writing in the widest variety of cases. The first involves becoming aware of the inner conflicts we experience when we write, and learning ways to reduce them to manageable levels. The second technique requires setting up a schedule of daily writing and giving yourself rewards or punishments depending on how you meet your requirements. Even though the latter method lacks the mystery or magic we would like to associate with effective cures, research has shown it to work in just about any case, producing the largest and most long-lasting increases in productivity and creativity.

By combining the two techniques, you can diagnose the conflicts that inhibit your writing, then reduce their intensity, and increase the amount you write and the ease with which you write it.

LOOSE LIPS SINK SHIPS

Some of you may not be aware of the fact that you argue with yourself while you are writing. But if you slow down and listen to your thoughts the next time you write, you will notice at least two voices, maybe more, that keep up a running commentary about what you're writing. As an example, let's take another look at Valerie, the student who has such a hard time starting her papers.

Valerie thinks of a possible first sentence and starts to write it down, but another thought interrupts with, "That's not

very interesting. Your first sentence needs to grab the reader."
So Valerie rejects the first sentence and tries another. We can
see two parts of Valerie at work here, two voices, one that produces content ideas to be written in the paper, another that
judges whether or not the ideas are good enough to meet the
standards Valerie has learned in class or imposed upon herself.

Cognitive psychologists have labeled this kind of thinking
"covert speech" or "self-talk," and they help their clients recognize and modify it in order to get out of such negative states as
depressions or phobias. But even before psychologists named
and studied this phenomenon, writers and artists had recognized it and given the voices various names: the inner creator
and the inner censor, the artist and the critic, the writer and
the editor, and the idea generator and the judge.

Timothy Gallwey, a well-known tennis instructor and
author of *The Inner Game of Tennis,* personified these voices as
two inner selves: Self 1 (the "teller" self) and Self 2 (the "doer"
self). He claims that the key to improving any skill lies in
improving the relationship between the two selves. In Valerie's
case, the relationship between her inner writer and inner critic
is not a good one. Whenever her writer produces a thought,
her critic speaks harshly and too soon, keeping Valerie from
writing a single sentence. Only the fear of turning in a paper
late will motivate Valerie's judge to ease up enough for her to

write. No wonder Valerie never writes unless forced by class requirements.

How can Valerie or any of us improve this inner relationship so we can minimize the pain of these conflicts? First, we need to become aware of our self-talk. Many of us aren't even conscious of its existence, especially not as the voices of separate entities, and gaining consciousness is the necessary prelude to improving their relationship.

But first, a word of reassurance. These separate selves exist in everyone. All of us talk to ourselves, not just people with split personalities or other emotional problems. What's important for our purposes is to recognize our self-talk and use it to benefit our writing, not inhibit it.

SPYING ON THE ENEMY

The first step you can take is simply to listen to yourself (or selves). The next time you begin to write, keep a part of your mind out of the action and just listen to what happens. The voices start even before you begin to write, expressing the dread or depression you feel about having to write in the first place ("I have to write that history paper! What's the point, anyway? I'll just get another C."). Then, once you begin to think of the actual content of what you will write, notice how the focus of the voices changes, and you can see more clearly the separation of the voices' roles into a writer and a judge. Listen closely to what the judge says about the writer's efforts. See if the judge overwhelms the writer (and you) with negative statements. Note how the remarks make you feel.

CATCH THE TRAITORS ON PAPER

To get a clear picture of the effect of your inner dialogue, try to write it down. Roger Garrison, who developed the Garrison Workshop Tutorial method for teaching composition, devised a "split-page" method for catching the voices in writing. Take a sheet of paper and draw a line down the middle. On the left side of the page, begin to write your paper. On the right side, write the thoughts you have about what you are writing and the feelings these thoughts cause.

When you first begin, write all the worries, judgments, and misgivings you experience. The judgment side may fill up even before you have written a single sentence of the actual paper. That's fine. In fact, it's what you want. It will help you produce a graphic picture of the strong role your self-talk can play in making your writing a hard, painful task.

After you see that what you say to yourself inhibits your writing, the next step is to experiment with replacing some of the negative talk with more encouraging statements. I don't expect you to switch from negative to positive self-talk on your first try. You developed your present attitudes toward writing during a period of years, so they won't change after doing one split-page exercise. In fact, at first you should be content with simply observing the dialogue.

Next, as a modest first step, you could try adding a third voice, and call it your observing self, a neutral voice that will speak to your judge with realistic suggestions for change such as: "OK, maybe you are right. Maybe my first sentence stinks. But we've got to start somewhere, and this sentence will at least get us started. We can always come back later and write a better introduction, but if we don't get started we'll never finish."

If writing on a split page bothers you, list your judgment thoughts on a separate sheet of paper. Don't get bogged down with concerns over the format of the exercise. In fact, you may not even need to write down your thoughts. The point is to become aware of your self-talk and then gradually to talk yourself out of being so hard on yourself. Remember, research has shown that even small changes in the nature of self-statements can make writing less painful and more productive.

One word of warning: Once you experience how harshly your judge treats your writer, don't judge yourself harshly for judging yourself harshly. This would just discourage you further. Try to keep one part of your mind free of judgments, and forgive all of your selves for being who they are and doing what they do. Slowly, you'll get better at letting each have its own say at its own best time (writer first, judge later). But at first, it's a rough go, so don't be hard on yourself when you find it's hard to change.

THE BEST WAY TO PROCRASTINATE BEFORE BATTLE

So far in this chapter, we have concentrated on the effects of self-talk on the process of writing, and we have looked at ways to replace negative self-talk with encouraging self-statements. An interesting variation on this theme is provided by a study done at USC by Dr. Linda Bannister for her dissertation research.

In looking at differences between students with high writing apprehension and those with low writing apprehension, Bannister found that just about all the students in her study avoided the writing assignment, procrastinating for the full week until the paper was due before they actually began to write. But she found an interesting difference between the self-talk of the high and low apprehensives during the week. The students with high writing apprehension tended to report thoughts that were unrelated to the content of the assignment: worries about how much time they had left before the paper was due, fears about the grade they would make, etc. On the other hand, students with low writing apprehension reported thinking about the actual content of the paper they were going to write. For example, they would think of ideas from the assigned readings that they could use in their papers, or they would consider how to organize the material and how to begin the paper.

As a result, the low-apprehensive writers reported fewer problems with starting and writing their papers once they sat down to write, and they generally turned out better papers than the high apprehensives. This finding is similar to accounts from a wide variety of scientists, inventors, writers, and artists who give credit to their unconscious thought processes for many of their creative ideas and solutions to problems. Evidently, once you give your mind a problem and begin to think about it, your mind will continue to work on it even when you're not consciously involved, so that in the case of the students who had actively thought about content ideas, they had a store of ideas at their command when it came time to write.

There's a lesson here for you, too. In the days before your assignment is due, monitor your thoughts about the assignment. See if you can think more about the content of the assignment and less about the grade you'll make or the time left before it's due. If the paper requires comparison and contrast, begin thinking about similarities and differences between the objects or ideas to be compared. If the assignment requires an argument, begin to think about the pros and cons of the different sides of the argument.

You can do this at any time of the day or night. You don't have to be sitting at your desk with a blank sheet of paper in front of you. In fact, if you have a particularly boring lecture class, use the time you'd normally spend daydreaming and think instead about the ideas involved in your next paper. Then when you actually begin writing, you won't be starting off cold. The beauty of this system is that you won't put in any more time writing, but when you write, you'll have more to say and say it more easily. It's simply another way of working smarter, not harder.

REWARDS FOR DOING BATTLE

If you're a person who likes to put off writing until you feel like doing it, then I've got bad news for you. Research has shown this to be the least effective way to accomplish writing tasks. The most effective method involves setting up a schedule to write a moderate amount every day, then rewarding yourself when you follow the schedule or punishing yourself when you don't. This may seem forced or mechanical, and you might be afraid it will hurt your creativity, but studies by Dr. Robert Boice at Long Beach State University have shown the opposite to be the case. Not only will this system increase productivity, but such a regular, enforced schedule also stimulates creativity and results in a long-term increase in positive attitudes toward writing.

Here's how to do it. If you already tend to manage your time well, then simply establish a period every workday when you will write, regardless of whether you feel like it or not. Also establish a moderate amount to be written each period (200 to 500 words), and don't stop until you have written your quota. Stick to your schedule and institute the system of rewards and punishments I suggested above. The reward could simply be the feeling of accomplishment when you finish your writing for the day, while the punishment could be the feeling of disappointment if you fall short of your goal. For me it's enough motivation to know how good I feel when I write my daily quota and how bad I feel when I don't.

However, if you're not able to motivate yourself with such light consequences or by setting up your own schedule, you can create more serious rewards and punishments and involve

someone else in your plan: a friend, your instructor, a writing center instructor, or even a counselor at your school's student health center. Make a contract with one of these people that requires you to follow a daily writing plan or suffer the consequences. I'm sure you can figure out ways to reward yourself and follow through when you fulfill the contract. Punishments can range from not getting a shower to sending off a donation of $25 to an organization you hate. Sometimes, the act of setting up the contract with another person will provide the motivation you need to write regularly, especially if you fear the person's disapproval.

Whatever it takes to get you started writing on a regular basis, do it. Once you get used to this regimen, you'll have less trouble each day beginning to write, you'll write more and produce more creative ideas, and you may actually come to enjoy writing.

WALK BEFORE YOU RUN TO WAR

If writing is now painful for you, then the methods discussed in this chapter will help you make it less painful. However, when you begin to put them into practice, remember to take the following approach: Walk before you run. The success of these methods depends on attitudes of moderation and self-acceptance. When you monitor your self-talk, be satisfied at first with just becoming aware of what you say to yourself. Don't be discouraged if your negative self-judgments don't change overnight. Likewise, when you set up a writing schedule, try to accept the minimum daily output it takes to meet your course requirements. Don't overwhelm yourself with marathon writing sessions or unrealistic volume requirements.

And finally, if you find that you still procrastinate, regardless of how hard you try to overcome it, then accept your procrastination and make it work for you. Tell yourself that at some level it must work or you wouldn't do it. Then, when you finally have to sit down and write, don't criticize yourself for having procrastinated.

This may sound like a strange approach to take, but students who try it tell me it helps. They say that when they finally start, at least they aren't freaked out by their procrastination, because now it has become part of their expected behavior. Also, when they combine a "planned" period of procrastinating with thinking about the subject matter of the assignment, they have plenty of ideas to write when the deadline draws near, and this makes starting easier.

You may find that these attitudes of moderation and self-acceptance will help improve your feelings about writing and help reduce the dread of having to write. And with that reduction, as well as gaining in productivity and creativity, you could also improve your chances of making the higher grades that correlate with lower writing apprehension.

8

• •

THE LIFE OF A
WRITING WARRIOR

• •

That the impact of your army may be like a
grindstone dashed against an egg, use the
science of weak points and strong.

Sun Tzu
The Art of War

DON'T LET FEAR OF WRITING
DECIDE YOUR FUTURE

A person I know, let's call him Bill, is an executive with a large
energy company. When Bill was fresh out of an Ivy League college with a degree in economics, he was hired as an economic
analyst by the CIA. The first time Bill's boss read a sample of
Bill's writing, he told Bill it was lousy, and if it didn't improve
in six months, Bill would lose his job.

Scary proposition, right? Doesn't this mean you'll have to
avoid careers that involve writing, and bosses who think your
writing is lousy? Maybe not. Listen to what happened: Bill's
boss told him that for six months, during working hours, Bill
would do nothing but write. So, Bill wrote for six months and
kept his job.

Of course *we* know that Bill's writing may not have been
"lousy" in the first place, especially if he could graduate from
the Ivy League. From reading about the research on grading, we
know that Bill's boss *perceived* Bill's writing as lousy, while

someone else may not have thought so. And yet, remember this: Bill "improved" his writing, and his boss kept him on in the job.

Here's another story from Bill. An executive in Bill's company, like the younger Bill, was a "lousy" writer. But now, the roles were reversed. Bill was the man's boss, and repeating history, Bill encouraged the man to improve his writing. In this case, however, the man didn't take Bill's advice, and thus was passed over for promotion. So he quit Bill's company and found a higher-paying job in a company where his duties didn't include writing.

As a final example, I give you my friend, Marty Greenberg. When Marty was a freshman pre-med student at UCLA, his English teacher gave him D's on his first papers, telling him, "I know you try hard, Marty, but you just can't write." Marty used many of the strategies described in this book (conferences, rewriting papers, conscientious classroom practices, etc.) and raised his grade over the course of the semester to an A. He went on to complete college and medical school, and then he became a child psychiatrist. He has published numerous research articles in medical journals, and he is the author of *The Birth of a Father,* a nationally known book on fathering. Not bad for someone who "just can't write."

I give you these examples to convince you not to let writing push you around when you choose majors and careers. You may think it's your weak point now, but you can turn it into a strength. Even in worst-case situations, you still have alternatives, and it's not necessary to give up your dream of a career just to avoid writing. Just avoid notorious teachers ("Two mistakes, and you get an F!"), and use the strategies from this book when you absolutely have to take one of their courses. Who knows, you could even end up a published writer, regardless of the career you follow.

TWO FINAL BATTLES TO INSPIRE AND GUIDE YOUR LIFE

More years ago than I care to admit, I too was a freshman, facing freshman English at Vanderbilt University. During orientation week, I took the English placement exam and tested into a section of "advanced" freshman English. This didn't surprise me too much. I had enjoyed English in high school and had done well, even winning one of the annual writing awards given by the National Council of Teachers of English to high school seniors.

What did surprise me was the D– I received on my first paper in freshman English at Vanderbilt. I stayed after class and tried everything that I advised you not to try to get your instructors to change your grade. I told my instructor about my experience and status as a writer. I argued over the grade. I probably even whined and begged. All to no avail. The grade remained the same. Then I asked the instructor to go over the paper with me, which he did, point by point, telling me how to improve it. I took it back to my dorm, rewrote it, and scheduled an appointment with my instructor, during which he pointed out further improvements I could make. I followed this

process for every paper, and the grades they received gradually improved until I ended up with A's on my last few papers and an A in the course.

I don't remember how I explained the jump from a D– to an A in one semester. In those days, I wasn't aware of the research on the subjectivity of grading, so I either thought my writing really had improved or that my instructor had rewarded all that extra effort, or a combination of the two. I do remember that I felt less confident as a writer, a feeling that

grew as I took more courses that required essays or essay exams, and I could never predict what grades my essays would receive.

I learned that grades on writing were unpredictable, and that I should avoid courses that required writing, and I also learned I could improve my grade by working extra and conferencing with the teachers. These are the essential lessons of this book, and their central message involves the issue of control. How do you gain control over your grade after the subjective system of grading takes it away?

We have answered that question in a variety of ways. You know how to stay away from the system whenever necessary, and you know how to use the system to your advantage. Best of all, most of the strategies you have learned don't require you to work any harder, just smarter.

We examined research that shows how animals and humans will give up trying a course of action when they become convinced they have no control over their situation. Students, when faced with the uncontrollable nature of grades on their writing, will also give up. But now you know you can exert control over your situation in writing classes, and that many of the actions you can take require no extra work, just extra awareness. The message is, you can do it, and you can do it without knocking yourself out trying.

Buckminster Fuller, one of the most productive inventors and architects of the 20th century and a revolutionary thinker in his own right, once experienced the failure of a small business he had started with the financial help of friends and family, losing everyone's investment in the venture. During that time, Fuller's first child died of a long and lingering illness. Feeling the extremes of helplessness and lack of control over his life, Fuller contemplated suicide. Faced with his death, he experienced the following thought: "I asked myself what a little, penniless human being could do for humanity that great corporations and great political states cannot do. Answering myself, I said: 'The individual can take initiatives without anyone's permission.'"

Of course, getting bad grades on your writing isn't as serious as financial failure or the death of a family member. Still, with your grade point average at the mercy of a subjective grading system, you may often feel like a small, helpless human being. Yet small, helpless humans can become strong guerilla writers. How? Like Fuller, you too can take initiatives without anyone's permission, and now you know which initiatives you can take to overcome the negative effects of the system. So, take them, and become a writing grindstone dashed against the egg of the grading system.

Good luck and good writing.

Bibliography

Bannister, L. A. *A Naturalistic Study of Composing Strategies Used by College Freshmen.* Diss. University of Southern California, 1982. *Dissertation Abstracts International* 43, 1436A.

Boice, R. "Psychotherapies for Writing Blocks." In *When a Writer Can't Write,* Ed. M. Rose. New York: Guilford, 1985.

Cazort, D. "Predicting Writing Apprehension (or Writer's Block) and Writing Quality of Undergraduate Students: A Review of Empirical Research." Unpublished manuscript.

Cazort, D. *Under the Grammar Hammer.* Los Angeles: Lowell House, 1992.

Daly, J. A. "Writing Apprehension." In *When a Writer Can't Write,* Ed. M. Rose. New York: Guilford, 1985.

Diederich, P. D. *Measuring Growth in English.* Urbana, IL: NCTE, 1974.

Gallwey, W. T. *The Inner Game of Tennis.* New York: Bantam, 1974.

Garrison, R. "Teaching Writing Effectively with Less Pain." A Workshop for Teachers of English Composition. Grossmont College. San Diego, CA. January 20, 1980.

Haynes, E. F. "Using Research in Preparing to Teach Writing." *English Journal* 67 (1978): 82–88.

Hillocks, G. "Synthesis of Research on Teaching Writing." *Educational Leadership* 44 (1987): 71–82.

Hollon, S. D., and Beck, A. T. "Cognitive and Cognitive-Behavioral Therapies." *Handbook of Psychotherapy and Behavior Change,* Eds. S. L. Garfield and A. E. Bergin. 3d ed. New York: John Wiley and Sons, 1986.

Kitzhaber, A. R. *Themes, Theories, and Therapy: Teaching of Writing in College. The Report of the Dartmouth Study of Student Writing.* New York: McGraw-Hill, 1963.

Krashen, S. D. *Writing: Research, Theory, and Applications.* San Francisco: Alemany Press, 1986.

Mao Tse-Tung. *Quotations from Chairman Mao Tse-Tung.* Peking: Foreign Language Press, 1967.

Parnes, S. J., Noller, R. B., and Biondi, A. M. *Guide to Creative Action.* New York: Scribner's, 1977.

"Rx: Journals. Dear Diary: You Help My Immune System." *American Health* Jan./Feb. 1987: 40.

Seligman, M. E. P. *Helplessness: On Depression, Development, and Death.* San Francisco: W. H. Freeman, 1975.

Seligman, M. E. P. *Learned Optimism: How to Change Your Mind and Your Life.* New York: Knopf, 1991.

Seligman, M. E. P., and Garber, J., eds. *Human Helplessness: Theory and Applications.* New York: Academic Press, 1980.

Sun Tzu. *The Art of War.* New York: Delacorte Press, 1983.

Taylor, W. F., and Hoedt, K. C. "The Effect of Praise Upon the Quality and Quantity of Creative Writing." *The Journal of Educational Research* 60.2 (1966): 80–83.

Wilson, K. G. "Is it 'Pnemonic' or 'Mnemonic'? 'Aberrant' or 'Aberant'? 'Seperate' or 'Separate'? *The Chronicle of Higher Education* 9 Dec. 1987: B2.

Appendix A:

RUBRIC AND SAMPLE GRADED PAPER

The following assignment generated the essays used in the study:

> Write a theme, 300–400 words in length, that proves one of the following points:
> TV is a wasteland.
> TV is not a wasteland.

See sample on the following page.

RUBRIC

In general, thoughtful, critical responses to the assignment will be placed in the upper half; in addition, those that demonstrate global organizational and argumentative skills will usually be rewarded over those that merely demonstrate sentence level competence.

T. S. Eliot Revisited

If you've ever stood in line at a supermarket you've experienced it. Inching forward, your eyes search frantically for reading material that will take your mind away from the price of beef. Aware that they have a slow moving, if not totally captive, audience the publishers of America have provided a host of visual delights. Racks and racks of newspapers and magazines reach out for our attention and money. Their shiny pieces of bait are television personalities.

Television personalities have become surrogate family members. The tragedy of this is compounded when the personalities provided by the television industry are two-dimensional, partly inane and totally boring. Television's ease of access gives these characters an omnipresence approaching that of minor gods.

Television is a technilogical development that is sixty years old yet still packs a lot of awe. The idea of pictures being transmitted through space has proven its ability to marvel generation after generation. For some unexplained reason, this wonder at the medium has spilled over onto the characters that it bears. Unfortunately, such wonder is rarely derserved.

In the early sixties, then FCC Commissioner Newton Minnow said he felt that television was a "wasteland." Minnow maintains that he only made this statement once. If so, then it has drawn life from its applicability.

Commercial television provides little more than a place for the witless, dull and huddled unimaginative masses to meet their peers. Chronic viewers are rarely those who thrive on challenge. Week after week they see petty folk acting out equally petty dramas with a gravity and spectacle that had hitherto been reserved for Mt. Olympus. With such saturating reinforcement, mediocrity has become synonymous with apple pie.

Perhaps the last stronghold of quality programming is the Public Broadcasting system. Yet in its continuing search, for donor dollars, PBS has resorted to a large number of dramas that bear some striking resemblances to their commercial counterparts.

In early 1980, former television network executive Fred Friendly said that the only worthwhile programming produced by the major networks was their news shows. If the same energy were applied to the balance of the programming perhaps the wasteland would bear a few flowers.

Handwriting Sample

If you've ever stood in line at a supermarket you've experienced it. Inching forward, your eyes search frantically for reading material that [crossed out] will take your mind away from the price of beef. Aware that they have a slow moving, if not totally captive, audience the publishers of America have provided a host of visual delights. Racks and racks of newspapers and magazines reach out for our attention and ...

Upper Half

An A or A– essay will:

- contain a clear purpose, a strong introduction (thesis sentence and/or paragraph), and a thoughtful conclusion;
- effectively recognize complexities, thoughtfully addressing more than one of them;
- contain strongly supportive details, a judicious sense of evidence;
- be logically developed and quite well organized;
- use a style and tone appropriate to the purpose;
- show mature sentence variety and paragraph development;
- be virtually free of grammar and usage errors.

A B+ or B essay will:

- contain a clear purpose, a strong introduction and conclusion;
- effectively recognize complexities, addressing more than one of them;
- contain supportive details, a good sense of evidence;
- be logically developed and well organized;
- use a style and tone appropriate to the purpose;
- offer adequate sentence variety and paragraph development;
- lack the verbal felicity or organizational strength of an A or A– essay.

A B– or C+ essay will:

- contain a clear purpose, a strong introduction and conclusion;
- effectively recognize complexities;
- contain supportive details, a sense of evidence;
- display competence in logical development and organization, although it may exhibit occasional organizational or argumentative weaknesses;
- use a style and tone appropriate to the purpose;
- display competence in sentence variety, paragraph development, grammar, and usage.

Lower Half

A C or C– essay will acknowledge the complexity of the issue, and attempt to address it, but will be weakened by one or more of the following:

- omit a clear purpose, thesis, or conclusion;
- be too general, or be too specific;
- contain trivial or frivolous points (or supporting material);
- have flaws in organization;
- fail to develop an appropriate tone;
- contain flaws in style, grammar, or usage.

A D+ or D essay will address the issue, but will be weakened by some of the following:

- be far too general, or be far too specific;
- contain a vacuous or trivial argument;
- have little controlling organization;
- have noticeable flaws in style, grammar, or usage.

A D– or F essay will be seriously flawed in terms of argument, organization, or usage.

Appendix B:

• •

ASSIGNMENTS FOR WRITING PRACTICE

• •

In choosing the following assignments, I kept in mind the method that research indicated to be the most effective practice for improving writing. Hillocks called it "inquiry" writing and defined it as writing that involves transforming data from its original form into your own words. The type of "data" can vary widely, from a scene you describe to a set of facts you use to argue the points of a controversial issue.

When choosing a subject, the most important consideration is whether or not it interests you. That doesn't mean you should spend hours trying to find a subject that is just right for you. Any of the subjects will give you the practice you need, and if you like the subject, you might begin to enjoy writing more.

Even if you're not excited about any of the topics, choose one anyway and write. This can be good practice to prepare for courses in which you'll be required to write on assigned topics that won't interest you. You could learn the trick of brainstorming about a boring topic until you find an angle that interests you. Then you can apply this skill to any writing assignment.

In my teaching experience, I have found that some students like to choose their own subjects, while others like to have specific topics assigned to them. So, I have provided a set of very general assignments that you can reuse repeatedly with different topics, and I have given a list of specific topics. Read through both lists, and you will probably find topics in every category that interest you. If not, then you may be suffering from writer's block, but don't let that worry you. Remember, you're in good company. As many as 80 percent of UCLA students share your aversion to writing, and as you found out in Chapter 7, you can do something about it. If necessary, reread that chapter and then come back to this Appendix for writing topics.

General Assignments

Pick an appropriate audience and a topic in one of the following categories, and write a 500-word theme.

1. Write a story about something that happened in your life and taught you a lesson.

2. Write a description of a person, place, or thing, and tell what is significant about it.

3. Write directions telling someone how to do something or make something.

4. Write an article explaining why you made one choice instead of another. Compare the alternatives that led to your choice: why you bought one product rather than another, chose one college rather than others, voted for one candidate over others.

5. Write a paper persuading someone to believe your position on a current issue or to take a course of action. A good source of topics for persuasive or argumentative papers is the opinion-editorial page of a

newspaper, especially *USA Today.* Each day, it treats a different issue and prints opposing arguments by experts on the subject. So at one and the same time, you can find good topics and read good models of persuasive writing.

Specific Writing Topics

I selected these topics from "A Thousand Topics for Composition: Revised," *Illinois English Bulletin,* Volume 58, No. 4, January 1971. To receive the full list, contact the *Illinois English Bulletin,* English Building, 608 Wright Street, Urbana, Illinois 61801.

Personal Reminiscences

1. My first fight.
2. My first encounter with racial discrimination.
3. My first job.
4. My most important decision and why I made it.
5. My most embarrassing moment.

Personal Reactions

1. The real me.
2. Why I will go to college.
3. My idea of hard work.
4. My idea of a perfect school.
5. What I would do with $100,000.

Familiar Essay

1. Let me cry on your shoulder.
2. What a home ought to be.
3. What it means to be poor.
4. Saturday night.
5. If we could read each other's minds.

Character Sketch

1. A person I have almost forgotten.
2. A person I can't bear.
3. My favorite teacher (relative, commentator).
4. My best friend.
5. A person who has influenced my life.

Description

1. The most beautiful spot I know.
2. A storm (snow, rain, dust, or wind storms).
3. The main street of my hometown (describing stores, people, landmarks, etc.).
4. Sounds at night.
5. The most horrible sight I ever saw.

Processes

1. How to spend a weekend.

2. How to be popular.

3. How to write a good theme.

4. How to prepare for an examination.

5. How to spend your time profitably while standing in line.

Comparison and Contrast

1. San Francisco versus Los Angeles as a vacation spot (or any two cities).

2. Effective and ineffective radio or television advertising.

3. Formal education versus business experience.

4. Evils and virtues of competition.

5. My school and the ideal school.

Persuasive Exposition

1. Everyone needs some kind of religion.

2. Be a nonconformist.

3. Don't count too much on first impressions.

4. Foreign customs we should borrow.

5. The best sport to watch.

Argumentative Exposition

1. English courses should not be required of all students.
2. Advantages of good business ethics.
3. Exams—good or bad ideas?
4. Why get married?
5. What our school needs most.

Sports

1. An outstanding sports event.
2. Are athletics physical education?
3. The nation's top basketball team.
4. Winter sports.
5. Women in sports.

The News—National and International

1. Do we need birth control?
2. Causes of Russia's suspicion of us (or vice versa).
3. Most interesting news story of the year.
4. Foreign influences in American life.
5. Racial (religious, social) prejudice in America.

Science

1. A modern invention.
2. Travel in the next decade.
3. A recent development in medicine.
4. Opportunities for a career in science.
5. How long can a car last?

The Arts and Entertainment

1. Interior decoration (color schemes, period furniture, etc.).
2. Schools of modern art.
3. Types of American architecture.
4. Movie villains—new style.
5. The best entertainment of the year.

Farming

1. The value of 4-H clubs.
2. Farms: the life of the nation.
3. The development of hybrid corn.
4. Development of hybrids.
5. What is the Farmer's Cooperative Association?

Religion

1. The place of religion in the world today.
2. Religion and life.
3. The basic teaching of my church.
4. Religion in school.
5. Does religion make sense?

Philosophy

1. The most important thing in life to me (values).
2. My philosophy of life.
3. My idea of the good life.
4. On death.
5. Truth.

The School

1. Social prestige in school.
2. What makes a course popular with students?
3. Interracial relations in our school.
4. Sex education should be compulsory.
5. A deficiency in American education.

Appendix C:

• •

A GUERRILLA WRITER'S HANDBOOK: WRITE SMARTER, NOT HARDER

• •

Free Writing

Key Problem:
For most of us, writing is a hard, slow process. We think about each word or phrase before we write it down, trying too hard to get it right. As a result, we often don't get anything down at all, or we scratch out what we do.

We need something to help us free the flow of our ideas and get them down without so many hesitations.

Suggestions:
One method that helps is called "free writing." If practiced regularly, free writing will help you write more in a given time, with greater ease, and even help you improve the quality of your writing. It's also called "wet-ink writing," because you write so quickly, you don't give the ink a chance to dry.

1. To start with, give yourself a time limit of ten minutes, and then start writing about anything at all. You can write for more than ten minutes, but not for less.

2. Once you start writing, don't stop. If you can't think of anything to say, write, "I

can't think of anything to say," or "I'm stuck, I'm stuck, I'm stuck," until you think of something to write.

3. Don't stop to think about correct spelling or punctuation. No one but you will ever read this, so don't worry about the quality of the writing or the social acceptability of the ideas. Just keep moving, and surprisingly, even though you give yourself permission to write poorly, you'll begin to find some of your best writing along with the bad.

4. Practice this a minimum of three days a week for ten minutes each day, and you'll soon notice a difference in the speed and ease of all the writing you do.

5. Also, before you write anything else, try free writing for five or ten minutes as a warm-up exercise. You could even try free writing the first draft of whatever you have to write, and then go back and rewrite it.

Remember:
Free writing will help free your writing hand. If you do it on a regular basis, you'll be able to perform any writing task with greater ease.

GETTING STARTED

Key Problem:
The first step in writing can often be the hardest one to take. The blank sheet of paper lying in front of you demands that you write something perfect, a good first sentence or introduction, something that will impress your readers. And that kind of demand is just what makes it so hard to begin writing.

Now, what can you do to make this first step easier?

Suggestions:

List making can be the key you need to unlock your ideas. Getting something down on paper, especially if it doesn't have to be in final form, will take you past the first obstacle to writing: the clean, white page.

1. Make a quick list of ideas about your topic: facts, opinions, comparisons—any ideas at all. This is a rough list of whatever occurs to you about the subject, in whatever words and whatever order it comes.

2. While you're making the list, watch for new ideas that the list itself will suggest. These ideas may also come later, at odd moments after you've put the work aside. Be receptive when they come, and note them down.

3. Don't worry about irrelevant ideas. They can help you make associations that will stimulate your thinking.

4. Once you finish your list, you'll be surprised at how helpful it can be. Often, after renumbering the order of the ideas for better organization, you can write a first draft using this list as an outline.

5. If you ever feel so blocked that you can't even make a rough list, try free writing for ten minutes, or go talk to someone about your ideas. Then write your list.

6. If you still can't get started, forget it and work on something else, or take a break and go to a movie. Never sit and stare at a blank page, unless you find that works to unblock you.

Remember:
The most important thing about getting started is getting started. Write anything, but write. With experience, you'll find that the act of beginning to write releases more energy for writing, but you have to begin to find that out.

HELP FROM CREATIVE PROBLEM SOLVING (CPS)

Key Problem:
Essentially, writing is the act of encoding your ideas in a permanent form for an absent audience. The amount of time and effort this act requires depends largely on the speed and ease with which your ideas occur to you. So, in order to cut down on that time and effort, you need a method that helps you generate ideas more quickly and easily.

Suggestions:
Research in CPS has shown that if you put off judging your ideas until after you've listed as many as you can, you can generate a larger number of them, more quickly, than if you judge each idea as it comes. Not only that, you'll find more ideas that result in better solutions to problems among the ideas you generate using deferred judgment.

1. Before judging the worth of any single idea, list all the ideas you can. You'll have initial reactions to any idea you list, but don't let that keep you from listing it. In fact, let that reaction suggest another idea. For instance, "Too expensive" suggests "Find something cheaper." List it.

2. If you think of ideas that contradict each other, list them both without deciding which is right. Together, two conflicting ideas can produce a third.

3. Go ahead and accept crazy or silly ideas. They can create a new perspective that allows you to see something you couldn't see with your normal, sane vision. Also, listing them keeps your ideas flowing.

4. Be prepared to have new ideas when you least expect them. Often, the ideas that pop into your head are the most valuable.

5. To open up your ideas, use images as well as words.

Direct Applications of CPS to Writing:

1. Practice in imaging helps you to make the transition from the real audience you have when speaking to the imagined, absent audience you're writing to.

2. When deciding what order your ideas will take in what you write, wait until you've listed them all. You could even wait until after you've written something about each idea to decide on the final order.

3. When revising at the sentence level, play with different ways of expressing an idea before you judge any of them. Write them down; look at them; read them out loud. Then decide which is best.

4. Also during revision, to get the right word, make a "ladder of options." For example:

glittered

The sunlight danced on the waves.

sparkled

5. When you don't know the spelling of a
   word, and you can't look it up, write the
   options to see which looks right.

Remember:
Resist the tendency to judge ideas too soon—resist the need to
"no." Stay open to new ideas. Keep listing. Expect surprises.

AUDIENCE-PURPOSE

Key Problem:
Whenever you speak, it's always to a specific audience—at least
one real person—and you usually have a specific purpose in
speaking: either to inform, convince, or amuse that person. But
all too often when we write for school, it's to no one in particular, and we have no particular purpose in writing. As a result,
this kind of writing is much less effective than speech, and it
sounds formal and unnatural.

Suggestions:

1. To help make your writing as natural and
   effective as your speech, always imagine a
   specific audience, and be conscious of your
   purpose in writing to them. That is, always
   be aware of your audience and why you're
   writing to them.

2. Once you know who you are writing to and
   why, imagine that your audience will ask
   you the following questions:

   a. What's your point?

   b. What do you mean by it? Explain it
      to me.

   c. Prove it. Convince me it's true.

These questions will help you generate ideas about what you have to say to your specific audience, in order to achieve your stated purpose.

3. Before you write anything, you could try speaking what you have to say, either out loud to yourself or to a friend, or try recording it on tape. Then write it.

4. Another good way to write to a specific audience is to imagine you have to write a speech, and then write it as you'd give it to a real group of people.

Remember:
The purpose of your writing is to explain something to someone in a convincing way. How you explain it depends on who you're explaining it to, so keep your readers with you in imagination, and write to them in the same direct words you'd use in speaking.

THE FIRST DRAFT

Key Problems:
In writing, the longest path to your goal can take you there in the shortest time. That is, it takes less time to write a messy, imperfect first draft and rewrite it than it does to squeeze out a single effort at a perfect paper. And since the act of writing generates ideas, you need a method of writing that will allow you to incorporate what's generated. A first draft is the place where you can do both: generate new ideas *and* incorporate them.

Suggestions:
Some writers call their first draft a "discovery" draft. Try thinking of yours in this way in order to loosen up your ideas and speed up your writing.

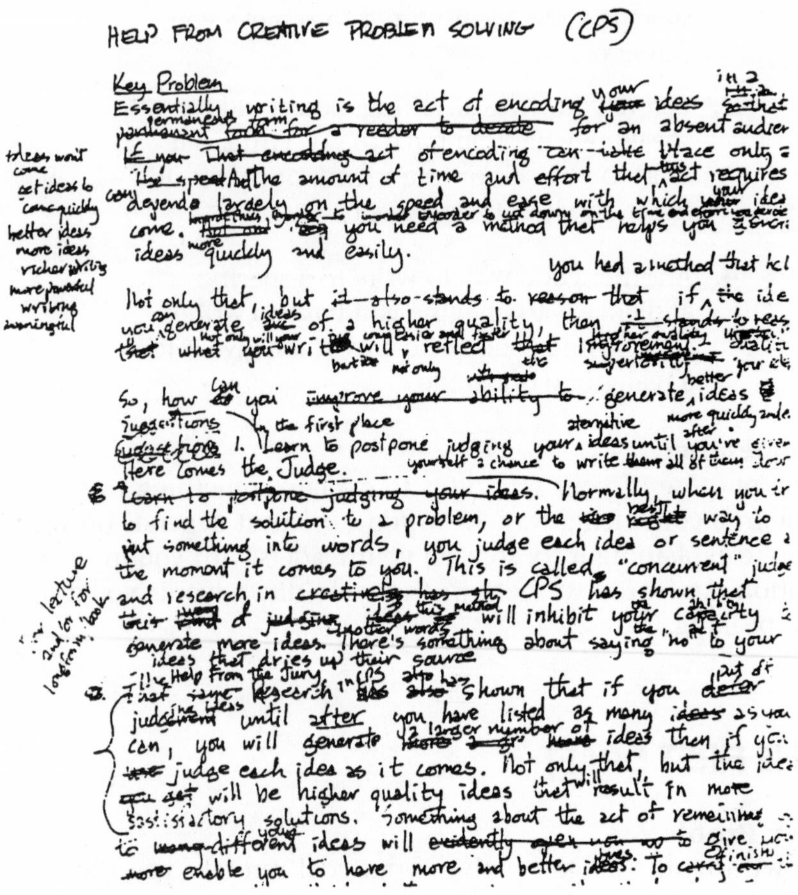

HELP FROM CREATIVE PROBLEM SOLVING (CPS)

Key Problem
Essentially, writing is the act of encoding your ideas in a
permanent form for a reader to decode for an absent audience
If you That encoding act of encoding can take place only as
the speed And the amount of time and effort that act requires
depends largely on the speed and ease with which your ideas
come. you need a method that helps you to get
ideas more quickly and easily.

(left margin notes:) ideas won't come / act ideas to come quickly / better ideas / more ideas / richer writing / more powerful writing / meaningful

you need a method that hel

Not only that, but it also stands to reason that if the ide
you generate are of a higher quality, then it stands to reas
that what you write will reflect that Improvement.

So, how can you improve your ability to generate ideas
suggestions in the first place.
Here comes the Judge.
1. Learn to postpone judging your ideas until you've given
yourself a chance to write them all down.

Learn to postpone judging your ideas. Normally, when you ir
to find the solution to a problem, or the best way to
put something into words, you judge each idea or sentence a
the moment it comes to you. This is called "concurrent" judge
and research in creative CPS has shown that
this kind of judging, ideas will inhibit your capacity t
generate more ideas. There's something about saying "no" to your
ideas that dries up their source.

(left margin, vertical:) in lecture and to book cover book

2. research in CPS has also shown that if you defer
judging ideas until after you have listed as many ideas as you
can, you will generate a larger number of ideas than if you
judge each idea as it comes. Not only that, but the idea
will be higher quality ideas that will result in more
satisfactory solutions. Something about the act of remaining
to many different ideas will evidently give you
more enable you to have more and better ideas. To finish

Sample First Draft

1. Begin wherever you feel you have the most to say or where your strongest interests lie. You could start in the middle or near the end, but above all, avoid getting stuck at the beginning, mired in the effort to write a good introduction. You can even save writing that for last. By then, you may have made "discoveries" that modify the point you wanted to make.

2. While writing your first draft, forget about correct grammar, spelling, and punctuation. Just keep moving until you've said all you set out to say. If you come to a word or punctuation mark that you aren't sure of, circle it and look it up later.

3. When new ideas come during the writing, or when you think of a better way to write a sentence, jot it down quickly and keep moving. Don't try to make anything perfect.

4. Remember to keep your audience in mind, and to write directly to her, him, it, or them.

5. Before you do any rewriting, give yourself a break from your first draft. It could last an hour or a day. During this break, be prepared for new ideas to come, and when they do, note them in writing.

6. Sometimes it helps to read your pre-writing lists and notes, and then to put them away before writing. Let your memory and intuition select what's most important. Then, after you finish the first draft, go back and reread your lists to see if there's anything you left out.

7. If you have the rare experience of your first draft coming out the way you want it to, *good.*

Remember:

Here are some slogans that apply to first draft writing. Before you begin, you can chant them quietly to yourself for encouragement:

Begin before you're ready.
False starts warm the engine.
Writing is discovery.

REVISION CHECKLIST

Key Problem:

Now that you've written a rough draft and you have something to revise, how do you achieve enough distance from your own writing to know what needs revising?

Suggestions:

Use the following checklist to put yourself into an imaginary reader's mind, and make the criticisms he or she might make:

1. Give your first draft a break before you revise it. This could last ten minutes or a day, but however long it is, be prepared for new ideas to come, and write them down when they do.

2. After your break, reread the paper and see if it really says what you wanted to say. Does it make the points you had in mind? Do you give examples to back up your points?

3. Read the whole paper out loud, or have someone read it to you. Does every sentence have the direct quality of your speech? Does every sentence "sound right"?

4. If something doesn't sound right, do this: Without looking at the page, speak the message of the sentence out loud, the way you'd say it to a real listener. Then use the spoken version that does sound right.

5. Use a dictionary to check the spelling of any words you're not sure of, and use a handbook to check punctuation or usage.

Remember:

Revision is the last step in the process of writing, and that's where you need to keep it. Forget about correctness until you've generated something substantial to correct, and then give it your undivided attention.

PUTTING IT ALL TOGETHER

Key Problem:

I have advised you to separate the steps of the process of writing, and in practice, you need to keep them separate. But separation doesn't imply any lengthening. When you put the steps back together, you'll find that the whole process takes less time and effort than before.

Suggestions:

Anytime you have something to write, try the following steps:

1. First, think of who your audience is, and what you want to say to her or him or them. Then write the name or names of the audience at the top of your first page, and below that write the purpose in communicating with them.

2. Keeping your audience in your imagination, make a quick, rough list of what you want to say to them. Just write a short phrase to remind you of each idea, and remember to defer judgment of any idea until you've listed all of them. Also, don't worry about the order of the ideas. List them in whatever order they come.

3. Now, read over your list and see what happens. Do you get any new ideas? If you do, list them as well. Also, you can begin reorganizing the order of your ideas. Either number the ideas in the order they'll come in your first draft, or write a rough outline. But don't get stuck trying to do the outline correctly. Concentrate on your audience and what you want to say, and the order will sort itself out.

4. Still imagining your audience, begin to write what you would say to them if you were talking. If you have a problem writing an introduction, you can write that later, when you have something to introduce. In fact, instead of beginning at the beginning, you could try starting wherever you have the most to say. Then once you're warmed up, you can go back and write the earlier sections.

   Remember, this is only a rough draft, so forget form; forget any maxims from composition; forget good grammar, punctuation, spelling, or correctness of any kind. You can always come back later and look all that up, but for now, keep writing and don't break your tempo. Give yourself permission to make mistakes, and go all out to say what you have to say to your audience.

5. When you've finished your rough draft, give it a break. Then go back and rewrite it, following the steps of the Revision Checklist.

Remember:

In writing, the longest way to your destination can get you there in the shortest time. Doing the steps separately speeds up the whole process.

PUTTING IT ALL TOGETHER (SUMMARY)

Key Problem:

I have advised you to separate the steps in the process of writing, and in practice, you need to keep them separate. But separation doesn't imply lengthening. When you put the steps back together, you'll find that the whole process takes less time and effort than before.

Suggestions:

Any time you have something to write, quickly go through the following steps:

1. Choose your audience and purpose and write them at the top of the page.

2. Make a quick, rough list of what you want to say to that audience.

3. Reread your list and write down any new ideas. Let your mind begin to reorder the ideas.

4. Imagining your audience, talk-write what you have to say. This is only a rough draft. Forget form, forget any maxims from composition. Give yourself permission to make mistakes, and just *write*.

5. When you've finished your rough draft, give it a break. Then go back and rewrite it, following the steps of the Revision Checklist.

Remember:

In writing, the longest way to your destination can get you there in the shortest time. Doing the steps separately speeds the whole process up.